easy vegetarian slow cooker cookbook

easy
vegetarian
slow cooker

125 Fix-and-Forget Vegetarian Recipes

ROCKRIDGE
PRESS

Photo Credits: Stockfood/Condé Nast Collection, Cover/p.2; Stockfood/Gräfe & Unzer Verlag /Rynio, Jörn, p.6; Stockfood/Foodografix, p.8; Stockfood/Mikkel Adsbol, p.10; Stockfood/Stockfood/ Snowflake Studios Inc., Back Cover/p.22; Stockfood/Bruce James, p.38; Stockfood/ Caggiano Photography, p.60; Stockfood/Snowflake Studios Inc., p.74; Stockfood/Shea Evans, p.92; Stockfood/Chugrad McAndrews, Back cover/p.114: Stockfood/Tanya Zouev, p.134; Stockfood/Jim Norton, Back Cover/p.156; Stockfood/ Foodcollection, p.180; Stockfood/Victoria Firmston, p.194

ISBN: Print 978-1-62315-552-0 | eBook 978-1-62315-554-4

Try These First!

Wake up to the tantalizing smells of
Overnight Cinnamon Buns. 57

Transport your taste buds with the flavor of
Indian Red Bean Curry. 70

Enjoy the tangy new spin that **Creamy Broccoli
and Blue Cheese Soup** puts an old classic. **83**

Savor a melt-in-your-mouth vegetarian favorite
with **Eggplant in Hoisin Garlic Sauce. 131**

Enjoy eating—or treating friends to the gift of—
this rich and sweet **Cheesecake in a Jar. 167**

Contents

Introduction

ANYONE WHO HAS BEEN A VEGETARIAN for any length of time has heard the questions from well-meaning friends and family: "What do you eat—carrot sticks and salad?" or "Where do you get your protein?" There are so many misconceptions about the vegetarian diet.

In all likelihood, you already know that vegetarians can eat a wide variety of food. There are vegetarian options at almost every type of restaurant, and nonmeat proteins like beans, nuts, grains, and certain vegetables make for delicious, hearty meals. From savory stir-fries to burritos, frittatas, pizzas, lasagna, and endless bowls of soup, vegetarian cuisine is healthy, filling, and incredibly diverse.

But, even vegetarians can fall into a food rut now and then. We're all hardworking, busy folks with more things to do than there are hours in the day. Like all people, vegetarians are looking for ways to eat healthy, delicious food that is easy on the budget and doesn't take a lot of time to make. We'd rather spend our time *eating* great food than *making* great food. That's where the slow cooker comes in. Like a (virtually free) personal chef, your slow cooker will toil for hours in the kitchen, creating healthy, cost-effective meals while you go about your day.

But wait. While it's absolutely true that slow cookers do the bulk of cooking for us, sometimes recipes steal time from busy home cooks on the front end. Many slow cooker cookbooks are full of recipes that require pre-cooking in one way or another, whether it's sautéing onions or toasting seeds. You won't find that in this book. We're taking the "fix and forget it" concept seriously. Slice, dice, or chop the ingredients, and you're done. It's as simple as that. The 125 recipes in this book demand only fifteen minutes or less of prep time and include a wide range of flavors and cuisines that will help debunk the myths that surround vegetarian cooking and eating. You don't have to live on carrots and salad alone. You don't have to rely on tofu as your only protein source. You don't have to spend hours slaving in the kitchen to make three meals a day. Before long, you'll be savoring Chocolate-Hazelnut Banana French Toast, Vegetable Tikka Masala, Midsummer Night's Stew, and Perfect Pound Cake. Oh, the suffering! And the best part? Your slow cooker really will do all the work.

Are you ready to get slow cooking? Let's go!

A Fast Intro to Slow Cooking

WE LIVE IN A "FAST" society, where most things can be procured with the click of a mouse or a drive by the take-out window. But wanting everything so quickly comes at a price. Very often, when we're so focused on "fast," we lose the ability to savor. Recall, instead, the feeling of anticipation—the excitement of looking forward to something wonderful that is waiting ahead.

When you cook with a slow cooker, you get the best of both worlds. You get meals that are fast and easy but that also give you time to savor the anticipation. All day long you look forward to what's cooking, and then you return home to the aroma of a fully cooked meal.

In this chapter, you will get to know your slow cooker and learn the benefits of slow cooking, the best way to store leftovers, and the basics of food safety.

Five Reasons to Get Slow Cooking

There are many reasons to embrace the art of cooking slow. Not only does the slow cooker require very little prep, but it also does most of the work for you. And the long cook time encourages you to savor the anticipation of a wholesome, delicious, home-cooked meal. In case you're still not convinced, here are five more benefits of slow cooking that you might not have thought of:

1. **It can free up your time for better things.** Slow cooking is not just for busy weekdays. Set up your slow cooker on Saturday morning and relax all day while it does its thing. Spend time with loved ones. Go shopping. Read a book. Then enjoy a virtually effortless meal at the end of the day.

2. **It's healthier and less expensive than buying prepared foods, eating out, or having food delivered.** Slow cooked meals tend to call for cheap ingredients such as dried beans, grains, and root vegetables, which can withstand the extended cooking times. And since the flavors have lots of time to meld and intensify, there's no need for unhealthy additions like sugar, excess salt, and butter or oil.

3. **It's perfect for making big batches of vegetarian staples to keep on hand.** For quick vegetarian meals throughout the week, it helps to keep ready-made caramelized onions, marinara sauce, cooked beans, and vegetable stock in the fridge or freezer. In a slow cooker, these mainstays come together with minimal effort.

4. **It can help you stock your freezer.** The large size of most standard slow cookers makes it easy to plan "intentional leftovers." Make more than you need and freeze the rest so you'll always have something vegetarian in the freezer.

5. **It keeps the kitchen cool on hot summer days (and nights).** It might be bubbling on the inside, but your slow cooker will keep the heat contained much better than your stove or oven will. Just throw in the ingredients, turn it on, and find a pool to sit by for the rest of the day.

HEALTHY VEGETARIAN MEALS: A CLOSER LOOK

Pop quiz: What do the following foods have in common: Oreos, French fries, potato chips, diet soda, Pop-Tarts, and refrigerated crescent rolls? The answer? They're all vegan.

Clearly, just because something is vegetarian or vegan doesn't mean that it's healthy. Many processed and sugar-laden "foods" don't contain animal products but are by no means good for you.

In the recipe chapters that follow, you won't find any processed "fake" foods. Granted, some of the recipes are healthier than others, but every recipe in this book is made with meatless whole foods cooked in a way that retains their inherent nutrients. Beans, whole grains, vegetables, fruits— these are the staples of a healthy vegetarian diet.

Now, with this book, you are armed with 125 delicious and nutritious vegetarian recipes to choose from. And, since each recipe includes nutritional information, if you're watching your intake of certain things (fat or carbs, for example), you can choose the recipes that best fit your lifestyle.

Let's talk for a bit about the idea of "fat." These are not necessarily "low-fat" recipes (although some are naturally low fat). Just like there's a difference between "vegetarian" and "healthy," there's also a difference between "fat" and "unhealthy." Our bodies need certain types of fat to function, such as those found in olives, avocados, and other plant sources. But as with all things, when you eat one meal with high-fat content, even if it comes from good and natural foods, make sure to balance your other meals in the day with leaner recipes.

Slow Cooker Basics

Although slow cookers are incredibly easy to use, it's still a good idea to understand some fundamentals before you get started. Many a novice slow cooker chef has waited hours and hours only to discover that he or she made a basic error and the end result was inedible. In this section, you'll learn everything you need to know to avoid mistakes and ensure delicious results.

SLOW COOKING VERSUS STOVETOP AND OVEN COOKING

Simmering, steaming on the stove, and braising in the oven are techniques that require long cooking times, but not nearly as much time as the slow cooker requires. So what's different about making food in a slow cooker?

Slow cookers are electric appliances designed to cook foods for long periods of time using low, moist heat. The typical model consists of a stoneware or ceramic "crock" set inside a heating element with a dial that has at least two settings: low and high. The lid traps in steam, flavors, and nutrients and forms a seal with the crock insert to maintain a constant, steady temperature. Once on, the slow cooker heats up quickly to bring the food above the "danger zone"—40°F to 140°F—in which bacteria can grow. Then it maintains a stable temperature (about 200°F on low and about 300°F on high) until the food has finished cooking, anywhere from four to ten hours. In this low-heat, moist environment, beans and grains are cooked to perfection and dense root vegetables will melt in your mouth.

Stovetop slow cooking can be done in stockpots, multi-pots, saucepans, and Dutch ovens.

» *Stockpots* are tall, straight-sided stainless steel pots ranging from 8- to 20-quart capacity. They are designed to heat rapidly and simmer long and evenly, and they are mostly used to make homemade stock, hence the name.

» *Multi-pots* are almost identical to stockpots, but with a slightly smaller capacity (ranging from 6 to 12 quarts) and a heavier base. They have tight-fitting lids and come with two perforated inserts: a large one for cooking food in water and a smaller one for steaming food above water. These pots are ideal for smaller batches of stock, soups and stews, steamed vegetables, and pastas and grains.

» *Saucepans* are heavy, flat-bottomed pans with tall vertical sides and long stick handles. They are great for simmering sauces, poaching eggs, and cooking pasta and grains.

» *Dutch ovens* are similar in shape to multi-pots, but are made from heavy cast iron (sometimes covered in a coating of enamel). They come in a range of sizes—from 2 to 10 quarts—and they can be used on the stovetop, in the oven, or even over a fire. Dutch ovens heat slowly but hold that heat for a long time, making them ideal for stews and braises.

SLOW COOKER SIZES

Slow cookers come in a variety of sizes, from 1½- to 8½-quarts. The smallest ones are perfect for dips and sauces, and the largest ones are best suited for double batches of stocks or stews. The recipes in this book are all designed for 5- to 6½-quart slow cookers with oval inserts. This way, you won't need to have more than one slow cooker and the pot will be big enough to accommodate any recipe.

HOW THE SLOW COOKER WORKS

The slow cooker works by inserting a ceramic insert into a metal casing with a tightly fitting lid. The casing contains electrical coils that allow the food to be cooked slowly and evenly. Because the amount of electricity is so low, it is safe to leave it on overnight or while you're away from home.

Be careful not to overcook your foods, though. This means following the recommended temperature settings on all recipes. Also, it's important to get to know the unique characteristics of your slow cooker. The age, model, and heating variations of your cooker, paired with the altitude of your home and even the weather outside, can impact the cooking time for certain recipes. Make sure you test your food for doneness before serving, just in case, and adjust the cooking times as needed.

The temperature inside the slow cooker ranges from 200°F on the low level to 300°F on high. Many have a "warming" feature that stops cooking at a preset time and then keeps the food warm until you're ready to eat.

FOOD CONSIDERATIONS

Some ingredients are more suited to slow cooking than others. For instance, hard root vegetables, dried beans, and grains benefit from moist, lower temperatures and longer cooking times, while this same method reduces pasta to a gummy mess, turns tender vegetables like zucchini and peas to mush, and causes dairy products to curdle. If you are creating your own recipe, adapting a stovetop recipe for the slow cooker, or making substitutions to an existing slow cooker recipe, just follow these simple guidelines for the best results.

BEANS: Use dried beans, never canned, and soak them overnight before cooking. (If you only have canned beans, add them to the slow cooker in the last 30 minutes of the cook time.) Add sugar, salt, and acidic ingredients like vinegar or lemon juice only after the beans are tender, as these ingredients can prevent the beans from softening.

CITRUS JUICE: Bright flavor-enhancers like citrus juice should be added last, so they don't get lost in the other flavors of the recipe.

DAIRY: Dairy products such as milk, cream, yogurt, and sour cream will curdle when cooked for long periods of time. To prevent an unpleasant texture and flavor, stir them in toward the end of the cooking time.

HERBS AND SPICES: Many dried herbs and spices can get lost in slow-cooked meals. For the best results, add a small amount in the beginning of the cooking cycle, then taste the dish and add more as needed toward the end. However, some spices will intensify over time, such as chili and garlic powders, black pepper, paprika, cinnamon, cumin, cardamom, and coriander. Use these sparingly and adjust the recipe according to your taste. Fresh, leafy herbs such as basil, mint, cilantro, and parsley are best when added to the finished dish, while heartier fresh herbs such as rosemary, sage, and thyme can hold their own during slow cooking.

OATS AND GRAINS: Though quick-cooking and old-fashioned oats can be used interchangeably in many stovetop and oven recipes, the old-fashioned and steel-cut varieties are much better for the slow cooker, as they retain their shape during long cook times. Similarly, instant rice should be avoided in slow cooker recipes, as it will break down into a mushy, gruel-like consistency.

PASTA: If you want to add any kind of pasta (including couscous and orzo) to your slow cooker recipe, cook it on the stovetop according to the package directions and

MUST-HAVE PROTEIN SOURCES

One thing that most vegetarians get sick of hearing is, "Where do you get your protein?" There's a common misconception that humans need animal protein in order to be healthy. Everyone needs protein, but there are myriad ways to get it from plant sources. Here are some must-have sources of vegetarian protein. You'll find recipes containing all of these in this cookbook.

» Cheese (8g per ounce)

» Chickpeas (7.3g per cup)

» Eggs (6g per egg)

» Green peas (7.9g per cup)

» Lentils (18g per cup)

» Quinoa (8g protein per cup)

» Rice and beans (7g per cup)

» Steel-cut oats (6g per cup)

» Sun-dried tomatoes (4g per ounce)

Perhaps you noticed that a couple of popular foods made from soy, such as tofu and tempeh, are not on this list of essential nonmeat proteins. Though soy is a wonderful source of protein, a lot of vegetarians are concerned about its manipulation and overuse in many packaged and processed foods, such as meat substitutes, protein bars, cereals, bottled dressings, mayonnaise, and fast foods. Today, many people, and vegetarians in particular, eat an incredible amount of soy, and most of the time unknowingly. Though organic, non-GMO (genetically modified organism) soy products are perfectly healthy for otherwise healthy people when eaten sparingly, we omitted them from the recipes in this book in favor of other, less controversial proteins.

Because soy sauce is generally used in very small amounts, it is called for in some of the recipes in this book. If you wish to omit all soy from your diet, an excellent replacement for soy sauce is tamari. For those who are on a gluten-free diet, it is worth seeking out tamari specifically labeled "wheat-free."

stir it in just before serving. If you add it at the beginning with the other ingredients, it will transform over time into a sticky mess.

VEGETABLES: When choosing vegetables to include in your slow cooker recipe, think about how they will cook. Place root vegetables like carrots, potatoes, and winter squash in the bottom of your slow cooker, since they tend to cook the slowest, and chop your vegetables as uniformly as possible, so everything cooks evenly. If you prefer certain vegetables crisp-tender, like bell peppers, for instance, toss them in during the last 30 minutes of cooking. The same goes for any delicate, tender vegetables, such as peas, green beans, and summer squash: Add these at the very end of cooking to prevent them from losing their flavor and shape.

TO PREP OR NOT TO PREP

There are two kinds of preparations one might do when slow cooking. There are the necessary preparations, such as chopping and peeling. And then there are the optional preparations, such as sautéing or roasting the vegetables. Please note that the recipes in this cookbook don't require the optional cooking techniques. But, if you have a bit more time, most slow cooking experts agree that sautéing some vegetables (such as onions and garlic) before putting them in the slow cooker adds depth and complexity to the dish. Whenever the recipe would benefit from one of these techniques, it is identified in the headnote.

Freezing and Storing

One great thing about using a 5- to 6½-quart slow cooker is that you will probably have leftovers. Here are a few tips for storing any extras:

» Casseroles, soups, stews, and chili will all keep well in the freezer. Foods with soft potatoes, milk, cream, and other dairy will not.

» To freeze stews, braises, and other semi-liquid dishes with some fat content, first chill them completely in the fridge, then skim the fat from the top. Fat spoils over time in the freezer and shortens a dish's frozen shelf life.

» To keep food safe, cool freshly cooked dishes quickly before freezing. Putting foods that are still warm in the freezer can raise the freezer's temperature, causing surrounding frozen items to partially thaw and refreeze, which can alter the taste and texture of some foods. Place leftovers in a shallow, wide container and refrigerate, uncovered, until cool. To chill soup or stew even faster, pour it into a metal bowl set in an ice bath (a larger bowl filled halfway with ice water). Stir occasionally.

Food Safety

Here are some tips for safe slow cooking:

» Thoroughly wash your cooker, utensils, work area, and hands before and during food preparation.

» If you cut up vegetables in advance, store them separately in the refrigerator until cooking time. It will take some time for the slow cooker to reach a safe, bacteria-killing temperature, and the longer ingredients sit out at room temperature, the greater the risk of contamination.

» Store leftovers in shallow, airtight containers and refrigerate them within two hours after the cooking is finished.

» Do not reheat leftovers in your slow cooker. Instead, reheat cooked food on the stove, in the microwave, or in the oven and then place it in the slow cooker on the warm setting until you are ready to eat.

» If you return home to discover that the power went out during the slow cooking process, throw away the food, even if it looks fine. If you are at home when the power goes out, finish cooking the ingredients immediately on an outdoor grill or gas stove.

Using Your Slow Cooker: Dos and Don'ts

To make things simple, here are some dos and don'ts for successful slow cooking:

DO use ingredients that are about the same size so they cook evenly.

DO fill the slow cooker at least half and no more than three-quarters full. Under- or overfilling can affect the quality of the food.

DO wait until the last hour to add dairy ingredients, as they will curdle. Same thing with soft vegetables like spinach, zucchini, peas, and cooked pasta.

DO use wooden, plastic, or rubber utensils instead of metal so you don't scratch the slow cooker insert.

DON'T start with frozen ingredients. It significantly affects the time the slow cooker takes to heat up and extends the cooking time. That said, one recipe in this book does call for a frozen vegetable—okra—because it's worth the extra time to start with frozen. It's too easy to overcook fresh okra.

DON'T lift the lid when cooking. Some say that lifting the lid extends the cooking time by 20 minutes each time you do it. It's tempting, but try your best to resist the urge.

DON'T preheat the slow cooker. Adding cool ingredients to a hot slow cooker can crack the insert.

DON'T add too much liquid. The slow cooking process releases a lot of moisture, so adding too much liquid will dilute the recipe.

TOPPINGS TO TRY

By mixing and matching your slow cooker dishes with sauces and other toppings, you can create an endless variety of flavors in your meals. Here is a list of delicious toppings to try with some of the recipes in this book.

HOT SAUCES: Whether you prefer Sriracha, sambal oelek, Frank's Red Hot, Tabasco, or *Homemade Hot Pepper Sauce* (page 183), a touch of spice is really nice on beans or in soups and stews. Try *Tres Frijoles Chili* (page 97) with a dollop of hot sauce.

NUT SAUCES: Cashews, peanuts, and almonds all make excellent sauces to drizzle over steamed or sautéed vegetables or on grain dishes. Try *Garlic Cashew Cream Sauce* (page 185) drizzled over *Black Bean and Spinach Enchiladas* (page 121).

FERMENTED VEGETABLES: Refrigerated, preservative-free sauerkraut, kimchi, and other naturally fermented vegetables add a natural probiotic to a meal and a tremendous amount of flavor. Try topping *Lazy Lentils* (page 32) with kimchi or sauerkraut.

TAHINI-LEMON SAUCE (page 188): This tangy and rich condiment is common in Middle Eastern cooking. Use it to top *Chickpea and Mushroom Stew* (page 101).

TAPENADE: Skip the oil and add a simple olive tapenade to your favorite beans and greens dish. Traditional tapenade is a paste or dip with black olives, capers, and anchovies. To make a vegan version, combine finely diced black and green olives, capers, garlic, and freshly squeezed lemon juice. It's perfect on *Smoky Farro with Peas* (page 153).

SALSA: Whether you use store-bought or make your own *Custom-Designed Salsa* (page 189), it's fantastic served over Mexican dishes, like *Black Bean Burritos* (page 150), or as a topping for *Tres Frijoles Chili* (page 97).

PESTO: Good jarred pesto can be found in just about any supermarket these days, or make your own *Perfect Pesto* (page 191) and use it as a sauce on pizza or pasta or to add a boost of flavor to *Italian Minestrone* (page 80).

2
Unbeatable Basics
Beans, Grains, and Broths

Slow Cooker Bean Primer

MAKES ABOUT 7 CUPS | **COOK TIME** 8 HOURS | **LOW**

This is hands-down the easiest way to make beans. Who needs a can when you can cook your own from scratch? Cooked dried beans are more flavorful and less mushy than their canned counterparts, and they also enable you to control the sodium content of your finished dish.

1 pound dried beans, picked over and rinsed

Per cup: Calories 34; Fat 0g; Protein 2g; Carbohydrates 8g; Fiber 4g; Sodium 7 mg

1. Soak the beans in enough water to cover for 6 to 8 hours or overnight.

2. Drain the beans and place in the slow cooker. Cover and cook on low for 8 hours.

Tip: It's important to always soak your beans before cooking—especially red beans. Soaking them removes the enzymes that can cause digestive upset. Also, get familiar with your slow cooker to estimate the time needed for cooking. Older slow cookers may require cooking on high or cooking for longer. Newer ones may cook faster. The beans should be tender but not mushy.

Vegetable Broth

MAKES 3 QUARTS | **COOK TIME** 6 HOURS | **LOW**

A good homemade vegetable broth is a versatile ingredient to have on hand. You'll use it as a base for soups and stews or to add an extra layer of flavor to all sorts of sauces, grains, or beans. Fill ice cube trays with this broth so that you can have small portions to add to smaller recipes.

2 carrots, chopped

2 celery stalks, chopped

2 onions, chopped

1 large tomato, chopped

1 cup chopped mushrooms

2 or 3 garlic cloves, halved

2 bay leaves

¼ teaspoon salt (optional)

12 cups cold water

Per cup: Calories 17; Fat 0g; Protein 1g; Carbohydrates 4g; Fiber 0g; Sodium 69 mg

1. In the slow cooker, stir together the carrots, celery, onions, tomato, mushrooms, garlic, bay leaves, and salt (if using). Pour in the water.

2. Cook on low for 6 hours.

3. Strain into a large bowl, gently pressing the vegetables to extract the liquid.

4. Use immediately, cover and refrigerate for up to 5 days, or freeze for 3 to 4 months.

Tip: This recipe is also great for using up those leftover "scraps," like the ends of peppers, onions that are starting to sprout, and the like. Just make sure to peel everything first, or the stock might turn dark and bitter.

Simmered Marinara Sauce

MAKES ABOUT 6 CUPS | **COOK TIME** 8 HOURS | **LOW**

The secret to rich, hearty marinara sauce is cooking it all day. Making it in the slow cooker allows you to simmer your sauce for hours while you're away from the stove. Your Italian grandma would be jealous!

4 pounds fresh tomatoes, chopped

1 (6-ounce) can tomato paste

1 onion, chopped

2 or 3 garlic cloves, halved

1 tablespoon dried basil

½ teaspoon dried oregano

1 tablespoon firmly packed dark brown sugar

1 tablespoon balsamic vinegar

¼ teaspoon salt

Per cup: Calories 93; Fat 1g; Protein 4g; Carbohydrates 21g; Fiber 5g; Sodium 141 mg

1. In the slow cooker, stir together all the ingredients.

2. Cook on low for 8 hours.

Tip: Roma tomatoes are the classic type of tomato used in marinara sauce. But, if it's summer and you have fresh tomatoes from the garden, use those. The sweeter the tomato, the better the sauce! If seeds annoy you, take them out before adding the tomatoes to the slow cooker.

Asian Ginger Broth

MAKES 4 QUARTS | **COOK TIME** 8 HOURS | **LOW**

This delicious broth is great on its own as a simple soup, and it can also serve as the base for other Asian-inspired dishes. Add cooked noodles or tofu and top with sliced green onions or sliced mushrooms for a quick, healthy meal. This broth freezes well, so make a double or triple batch so you can have some on hand.

¼ **cup minced fresh ginger**

3 **tablespoons minced garlic**

2 **tablespoons grapeseed oil (or another neutral-flavored oil such as safflower or sunflower seed)**

¼ **cup plus 2 tablespoons cornstarch**

16 **cups cold water**

¼ **cup plus 2 tablespoons vegetarian bouillon base**

Per cup: Calories 80; Fat 5g; Protein 0g; Carbohydrates 7g; Fiber 0g; Sodium 2,603 mg

1. In the slow cooker, combine the ginger, garlic, and oil.

2. In a small bowl, whisk together the cornstarch and 2 cups of the water until dissolved. Add to the slow cooker.

3. Add the rest of the water and the bouillon base to the crock.

4. Cook on low for 8 hours.

Tip: Vegetarian bouillon can be found in many major markets where the regular bouillon is located. If you can't find it, you can substitute 16 cups of vegetable stock for the water and omit the bouillon.

Basic Brown Rice

MAKES 7 TO 8 CUPS | **COOK TIME** 6 HOURS | **LOW**

The slow cooker is even better than a rice cooker for making brown rice. The resulting rice has a deep nutty flavor and is extremely tender. If you want to cook the rice faster, set the slow cooker on high and reduce the cooking time to 3 hours.

Cooking spray

2 cups uncooked brown rice,
 rinsed and drained

3 cups water

½ **teaspoon salt**

_____

Per cup: Calories 172; Fat 2g; Protein 4g;
Carbohydrates 26g; Fiber 2g; Sodium 152 mg

1. Coat the slow cooker with cooking spray.

2. In the slow cooker, stir together the ingredients.

3. Cook on low for 6 hours.

Tip: You'll notice that the recipe calls for less water than is called for in stovetop recipes. This is because the slow cooker seals in the moisture. If you find that your rice is a little dry or is starting to get overcooked, add another ¼ cup of water and continue cooking on low heat until the rice is to your liking.

Mushroom Congee

SERVES 6 | **COOK TIME** 8 HOURS | **LOW**

Congee is a traditional rice porridge that is often eaten for breakfast in China and other parts of Asia. Sometimes it is cooked with vegetables, beans, or other add-ins, or it is made plain and served with side dishes or various toppings that diners can add to their liking. Common toppings include thinly sliced scallions, minced fresh ginger, fried shallots, chopped nuts, sesame oil, chili paste, tofu, or eggs.

1½ cups uncooked long-grain white rice

2 cups Vegetable Broth (page 26) or Asian Ginger Broth (page 28)

1 quart water

4 slices of fresh ginger, each about the size of a quarter

6 dried Chinese mushrooms, stemmed and finely chopped or crumbled

2 scallions

1 teaspoon salt

1. Combine the rice, broth, water, sliced ginger, mushrooms, scallions, and salt in the slow cooker.

2. Cover and cook on low for 8 hours, stirring occasionally, until the rice has softened and the soup is thick.

Per serving: Calories 199; Fat 1g; Protein 6g; Carbohydrates 41g; Fiber 1g; Sodium 652 mg

Crazy Simple Quinoa

MAKES 6 CUPS | **COOK TIME** 6 HOURS | **LOW**

Although we treat it like a grain, quinoa is actually the seed of a plant that is related to spinach, beets, and chard. It is an ideal food for vegetarians and vegans not only because it is super high in protein, but also because it is considered a complete protein, meaning that it contains all nine of the essential amino acids that our bodies need but cannot produce.

Cooking spray

1½ cups uncooked quinoa

1 tablespoon olive oil

3 cups water or low-sodium vegetable broth

½ teaspoon salt

Per cup: Calories 167; Fat 5g; Protein 6g; Carbohydrates 26g; Fiber 3g; Sodium 199 mg

1. Coat the slow cooker with cooking spray.

2. In the slow cooker, stir together the ingredients.

3. Cook on low for 6 hours.

Tip: *Quinoa has a bitter coating on it. Use a fine-meshed sieve to give your quinoa a thorough rinse before cooking.*

Lazy Lentils

MAKES 3 TO 4 CUPS | **COOK TIME** 8 HOURS | **LOW**

Lentils are a great source of protein for vegetarians. They don't need to be soaked before cooking, and they are filled with nutrients like iron, protein, folate, and manganese as well as fiber and "healthy carbs." For this recipe, you can use green or brown lentils, or a combination of the two.

1½ cups uncooked lentils, rinsed

4 cups Vegetable Broth (page 26), or store-bought

2 carrots, peeled and diced

1 onion, diced

3 garlic cloves, minced

½ cup golden raisins (optional)

½ teaspoon sea salt

¼ teaspoon freshly ground black pepper

2 tablespoons chopped Italian parsley

Per cup: Calories 375; Fat 2g; Protein 25g; Carbohydrates 65g; Fiber 24g; Sodium 1,027 mg

1. In the slow cooker, stir together the ingredients.

2. Cook on low for 8 hours.

3. Stir in the parsley just before serving.

Tip: When the lentils are cooked, stir in some coconut milk and freshly squeezed lime juice, if desired. You can also add in some peeled, diced sweet potatoes prior to cooking.

Set 'Em and Split Peas

MAKES ABOUT 3 CUPS | **COOK TIME** 4 HOURS | **LOW**

Split peas aren't just for soup. You can use them pretty much any-where you'd use lentils. This recipe provides you with plain cooked split peas that you can add to soups, stews, curries, or grain dishes as you see fit.

1¼ **cups uncooked split peas, rinsed**

4 cups water

¼ **teaspoon salt**

Per cup: Calories 280; Fat 1g; Protein 20g; Carbohydrates 50g; Fiber 21g; Sodium 216 mg

1. In the slow cooker, stir together the ingredients.

2. Cook on low for 4 hours.

Tip: *Split peas can get mushy if overcooked, which is why we stop the cooking here after 4 hours. Check them after the 4 hours are up, and continue cooking them on low heat if you like them softer.*

Unfried Rice

MAKES 6 TO 8 CUPS | **COOK TIME** 8 HOURS AND 15 MINUTES | **LOW**

This recipe is a healthy, delicious alternative to the greasy takeout version, and it's just as easy as ordering in. Feel free to add any other vegetables you like. Just make sure to add more delicate vegetables, like peas, toward the end of the cooking time so they don't get mushy.

Cooking spray

2 cups uncooked long-grain white rice

4 cups water

2 tablespoons olive oil

2 tablespoons soy sauce

1 medium yellow onion, finely diced

4 medium carrots, peeled and finely diced

½ cup frozen peas, thawed

Per cup: Calories 259; Fat 4g; Protein 5g; Carbohydrates 49g; Fiber 3g; Sodium 297mg

1. Coat the slow cooker with cooking spray.

2. In the slow cooker, stir together all the ingredients except the peas.

3. Cook on low for 8 hours.

4. Stir in the peas and let cook for an additional 15 minutes.

Tip: Drizzle the rice with sesame oil before serving to add a nutty flavor. For added protein, pour one or two lightly beaten eggs over the top after stirring in the peas and cook until the eggs are set. Stir and serve.

Kiss My Grits

MAKES ABOUT 6 CUPS | **COOK TIME** 6 HOURS | **LOW**

Grits are a Southern classic made from slow-cooked ground corn kernels. They are served sweetened with honey, maple syrup, or fruit for breakfast or topped with savory dishes like sautéed mushrooms or stewed vegetables for dinner. Let them cook overnight and you can wake up to a warm breakfast. Slow cooking makes them even creamier than the stovetop version.

Cooking spray

2 cups uncooked grits

6 cups water

1 teaspoon salt

Per cup: Calories 40; Fat 1g; Protein 1g; Carbohydrates 8g; Fiber 1g; Sodium 510mg

1. Coat the slow cooker with cooking spray.

2. In the slow cooker, stir together the ingredients.

3. Cook on low for 6 hours.

Tip: For extra flavor, add in ¼ cup heavy cream or 2 tablespoons unsalted butter during the last hour of cooking. Or, stir in ½ cup of Cheddar cheese.

Coconut Curry Simmer Sauce

MAKES ABOUT 3 CUPS | **COOK TIME** 8 HOURS | **LOW**

This sauce is so rich and full of flavor, you'll be tempted to eat it with a spoon. Serve it drizzled over sautéed or steamed vegetables—cauliflower, green beans, carrots, broccoli, you name it—and rice for a simple and satisfying meal. This recipe makes a mildly spiced sauce, but if you like it spicier, add more curry paste or powder.

2 onions, finely chopped

4 garlic cloves, minced

3 tablespoons minced fresh ginger

1 (6-ounce) can tomato paste

2 tablespoons ground cumin

1 tablespoon garam masala

1 tablespoon curry paste or powder

1 teaspoon red pepper flakes (optional)

2 cups unsweetened coconut milk

Salt

Per cup: Calories 519; Fat 43g; Protein 9g; Carbohydrates 35g; Fiber 9g; Sodium 96mg

1. In the slow cooker, combine all the ingredients, except salt.

2. Cook on low for 8 hours, and season with salt before serving.

Tip: There are many different kinds of curry. You can vary the flavor of this sauce by changing the type of curry you use. The Indian-style curry powders found in supermarkets, for instance, are usually made with a combination of dried and ground cumin, coriander, turmeric, fenugreek, and chiles, along with other spices. Thai curry pastes, on the other hand, usually combine lemongrass, kaffir lime leaves, galangal, and fresh turmeric root.

Sopa Mexicana

MAKES 6 CUPS | **COOK TIME** 8 HOURS | **LOW**

This simple vegetable broth is flavored with the classic Mexican flavor combination of cumin and oregano. It can be served as a simple soup or used as the base for many Latin-inspired dishes. Use it in place of water to make flavorful Mexican rice, or serve it with vegetables and homemade vegetarian "meatballs" in *Albondigas-less Soup* (page 91).

1 carrot, chopped

1 celery stalk, chopped

2 onions, chopped

1 large tomato, chopped

2 or 3 garlic cloves, halved

1 teaspoon ground cumin

½ teaspoon dried oregano

½ teaspoon salt

6 cups water

Per cup: Calories 28; Fat 0g; Protein 1g; Carbohydrates 6g; Fiber 2g; Sodium 214mg

1. In the slow cooker, stir together all the ingredients.

2. Cook on low for 8 hours.

3. Strain into a large bowl, gently pressing the vegetables to extract the liquid.

Tip: You can add a little more heat to the recipe by adding in a chopped jalapeño pepper. Also, for a brighter flavor, add some chopped fresh cilantro and the juice of 1 lemon in the last hour of cooking.

3

Breakfasts and Breads

Quinoa Hot Breakfast Cereal

SERVES 6 | **COOK TIME** 8 HOURS | **LOW**

Quinoa is the darling side dish of nutritionists and health food lovers, and it makes a fantastic breakfast cereal, too. It's got a nutty flavor and slight crunch. Even better, it's packed with protein to keep you full of energy until lunch. Here, it's sweetened with a bit of sugar and studded with raisins, but you can use any sweetener—maple syrup or honey would be delicious—or dried or fresh fruit that you like.

Cooking spray

1½ cups uncooked quinoa, rinsed

1 tablespoon grapeseed oil (or another neutral-flavored oil, such as safflower or sunflower seed oil)

3 cups water

½ teaspoon salt

½ cup raisins or other dried fruit

¼ cup granulated sugar

1. Coat the slow cooker with cooking spray.

2. In the slow cooker, stir together all the ingredients.

3. Cook on low for 8 hours.

Per serving: Calories 235; Fat 5g; Protein 5g; Carbohydrates 44g; Fiber 3g; Sodium 201mg

Creamy Overnight Steel-Cut Oats

SERVES 8 | **COOK TIME** 8 HOURS | **LOW**

This breakfast was made for cold winter mornings. Just set everything up the night before and you'll have warm cereal ready when you're hungry for breakfast. Steel-cut oats are a nutritional powerhouse food and are low on the glycemic index, which means they won't spike your blood sugar and they'll keep you satisfied for hours.

Cooking spray

2 cups steel-cut oats

4 cups water

¼ teaspoon salt

4 small plums, pitted and sliced

1 cup milk

Per serving: Calories 177; Fat 4g; Protein 7g; Carbohydrates 35g; Fiber 4g; Sodium 91mg

1. Coat the slow cooker with cooking spray.

2. In the slow cooker, stir together the oats, water, and salt.

3. Cook on low for 8 hours.

4. Spoon the oatmeal into bowls and add 2 tablespoons of milk to each. Garnish with the plums.

Tip: For added flavor and variety, add your choice of toppings—choose from butter or vegan margarine, milk or cream, almond or rice milk, cinnamon, fresh or dried fruit, or nuts.

Sunday Brunch French Toast

SERVES 6 | **COOK TIME** 8 HOURS | **LOW**

With this recipe, you can have your Sunday brunch and sleep in, too. If you also set the timer on your coffee maker, you'll have a virtually effortless morning meal. This French toast will more resemble a soufflé than regular French toast because it will puff up and get golden brown. Serve it with warm syrup, if desired.

Cooking spray

12 large eggs

2 cups whole milk

2 teaspoons ground cinnamon

2 teaspoons pure vanilla extract

2 tablespoons firmly packed dark brown sugar

1 loaf of sliced white bread

***

Per serving: Calories 409; Fat 15g; Protein 21g; Carbohydrates 46g; Fiber 2g; Sodium 684mg

1. Coat the slow cooker with cooking spray.

2. In a large bowl, crack the eggs and lightly beat them with a fork. Add the milk, cinnamon, vanilla, and brown sugar. Beat again for a few moments until everything is combined.

3. Dip each slice of bread in the egg mixture and layer the coated slices in the slow cooker. Pour any leftover egg mixture over the top.

4. Cook on low for 8 hours.

Chocolate-Hazelnut Banana French Toast

SERVES 6 | **COOK TIME** 8 HOURS | **LOW**

This recipe takes *Sunday Brunch French Toast* (page 43) to the next level with the addition of chocolate-hazelnut spread and bananas. The bananas will caramelize deliciously on the bottom of the slow cooker. The recipe calls for challah or egg bread, but you can substitute white bread if you prefer.

Cooking spray

4 bananas, sliced

1 loaf of challah or
   egg bread, cubed

12 large eggs

2 cups whole milk

2 teaspoons ground cinnamon

2 teaspoons pure vanilla extract

2 tablespoons firmly packed dark
   brown sugar

2 tablespoons chocolate-hazelnut
   spread (such as Nutella)

Per serving: Calories 516; Fat 17g; Protein 22g; Carbohydrates 69g; Fiber 4g; Sodium 692mg

1. Coat the slow cooker with cooking spray.

2. Layer the bananas on the bottom of the slow cooker.

3. Place the bread cubes on top of the bananas.

4. In a large bowl, crack the eggs and lightly beat them with a fork.

5. Add the milk, cinnamon, vanilla, sugar, and chocolate-hazelnut spread to the eggs and whisk for 2 minutes. The mixture will not be fully combined.

6. Pour the egg mixture over the bread cubes in the slow cooker.

7. Cook on low for 8 hours.

Apple-Cinnamon Risotto

SERVES 6 | **COOK TIME** 6 HOURS | **LOW**

Risotto makes a creamy and flavorful savory dish, but when sweetened with apples and brown sugar, it can be an extremely satisfying hot breakfast. For added texture and sweetness, you can stir in dried fruit along with the other ingredients. For added crunch and a bit of extra protein, serve it with a sprinkling of chopped nuts.

¼ cup butter

1½ cups Arborio rice

2 medium apples, cored and diced

1½ teaspoons ground cinnamon

⅛ teaspoon ground nutmeg

⅛ teaspoon ground cloves

¼ teaspoon salt

⅓ cup brown sugar, plus additional for serving

1 cup apple juice

3 cups milk

Per serving: Calories 383; Fat 11g; Protein 7g; Carbohydrates 65g; Fiber 3g; Sodium 215mg

1. Place the butter in the slow cooker and set it to high heat to let the butter melt.

2. Stir the rice into the melted butter in the slow cooker until all of the grains are nicely coated. Add the apples, cinnamon, nutmeg, cloves, salt, sugar, apple juice, and milk, and stir to mix well. Cover, turn the slow cooker to low, and cook for 6 hours. Serve hot, sprinkled with additional brown sugar if desired.

Tip: To make this recipe vegan, use vegan margarine in place of the butter and almond milk or another vegan milk substitute in place of the milk.

Grilled Cheese Monkey Bread

SERVES 12 | **COOK TIME** 1½ HOURS | **HIGH**

Monkey bread is a classic American recipe. It's most commonly a yeast dough that is formed into balls and pressed together in a tube pan after being dunked in melted butter and sugar so that when the loaf cooks, the pieces can be pulled apart. This savory version, in which the balls of dough are separated by cheese instead of butter and sugar, calls for refrigerated biscuit dough, but you can make your own if you've got the time.

Cooking spray

Parchment paper

2 (16-ounce) cans
  refrigerator biscuits

1 cup shredded Cheddar cheese

Per serving: Calories 278; Fat 14g; Protein 8g; Carbohydrates 31g; Fiber 1g; Sodium 840mg

1. Coat the slow cooker with cooking spray.

2. Line the bottom with parchment paper and then coat it again with cooking spray.

3. Take one biscuit and place one-twelfth of the cheese on it. Top with a second biscuit and pinch the edges together, making a ball. Repeat for the rest of the dough and cheese.

4. Layer the dough balls in the crockpot, overlapping as needed.

5. Cover and cook on high for 1½ hours or until the bread is puffed and browned.

Tip: You can make this vegan by using vegan cheese and dairy-free biscuits.

Mexican Tortilla, Egg, and Green Chile Casserole

SERVES 6 | **COOK TIME** 7 HOURS AND 20 MINUTES | **LOW**

Roasted green chiles and Cheddar cheese flavor this layered casserole. If you like a bit of spice in your eggs, add a diced jalapeño pepper to the egg mixture. Serve it with a dollop of *Great Guacamole* (page 190), *Custom-Designed Salsa* (page 189), or store-bought salsa.

Cooking spray

12 eggs

3 cups milk

3 cups shredded Cheddar cheese

1½ (7-ounce) cans roasted green chiles, drained

1 large red bell pepper, seeded and finely diced

1 onion, finely diced

2 cups fresh or frozen corn kernels

1 teaspoon salt

½ teaspoon freshly ground black pepper

12 corn tortillas, divided

Per serving: Calories 730; Fat 35g; Protein 39g; Carbohydrates 75g; Fiber 4g; Sodium 986mg

1. Spray the inside of the slow cooker with cooking spray.

2. In a large mixing bowl, whisk together the eggs, milk, cheese, chiles, bell pepper, onion, corn, salt, and black pepper.

3. Line the bottom of the slow cooker with 4 corn tortillas, tearing them as needed so that they cover the bottom completely. Pour half of the egg mixture into the slow cooker over the tortillas. Place 4 more tortillas on top of the egg mixture, tearing them as needed to cover completely. Pour the remaining egg mixture into the slow cooker and top with the remaining 4 tortillas.

continued >

Mexican Tortilla, Egg, and Green Chile Casserole, continued

4. Cover and cook on low for 7 hours. Remove the lid and let cook an additional 20 minutes. The edges will be lightly browned, and the cheese will have begun to get a bit crisp around the edges.

Tip: *For additional fiber and protein, replace the corn kernels with one 15-ounce can of drained black beans, or just add the beans to the casserole along with the corn.*

Fall Harvest Pumpkin Bread

SERVES 6 | **COOK TIME** 2 TO 3 HOURS | **HIGH**

As it bakes, this flavorful quick bread will fill your house with the scent of pumpkin and sweet fall spices, building the anticipation as it cooks. If you have any leftover bread, wrap it tightly in aluminum foil and keep it in the freezer for up to 3 months. It's the perfect thing to serve to drop-in guests around the holidays!

Cooking spray

2 cups unbleached all-purpose flour

1 tablespoon baking powder

½ teaspoon baking soda

¼ teaspoon salt

2 teaspoons pumpkin pie spice

½ teaspoon ground cloves

1 teaspoon pure vanilla extract

2 tablespoons water

1 cup pumpkin purée

½ cup molasses

½ cup honey

¼ cup coconut oil

Aluminum foil

1. Coat the bottom and sides of a 8-by-4-by-3-inch loaf pan with cooking spray.

2. In a large bowl, mix together the flour, baking powder, baking soda, salt, pumpkin pie spice, and cloves.

3. Add the vanilla, water, pumpkin purée, molasses, honey, and oil to the bowl and stir until just combined.

4. Pour the batter into the prepared loaf pan and smooth the top with a spatula.

continued >

Per serving: Calories 419; Fat 10g; Protein 5g; Carbohydrates 81g; Fiber 2g; Sodium 219mg

Fall Harvest Pumpkin Bread, continued

5. Crumple up 4 sheets of aluminum foil into balls and place them in the bottom of the slow cooker. Gently place the filled loaf pan on top of the aluminum foil so that the bottom of the pan is not resting directly on the bottom of the crock insert.

6. Cook on high for 2 to 3 hours, leaving the lid propped open with a wooden spoon. The bread will be done when a knife inserted in the center comes out clean.

7. Remove the bread from the slow cooker and let it cool for 5 minutes in the loaf pan. Run a knife around the edges of the bread and carefully invert it onto a rack to cool completely, about 1 hour.

Banana Nut Bread

SERVES 6 | **COOK TIME** 2 TO 3 HOURS | **HIGH**

This moist and delicious walnut-studded banana bread is a beloved classic, the kind of recipe that has been passed down for generations. Cooking it in the slow cooker, though, is a modern convenience that frees you from being chained to the kitchen while it bakes. Try it toasted and slathered with *Pear Applesauce* (page 159) or pumpkin butter for an extra treat.

Cooking spray

2 cups unbleached all-purpose flour

1 tablespoon baking powder

½ teaspoon baking soda

1 teaspoon ground cinnamon

½ cup granulated sugar

¼ teaspoon salt

1 teaspoon pure vanilla extract

2 tablespoons water

3 cups mashed ripe bananas (about 3 large)

1 cup chopped walnuts, divided

Per serving: Calories 409; Fat 13g; Protein 10g; Carbohydrates 68g; Fiber 5g; Sodium 205mg

1. Coat the bottom and sides of a 8-by-4-by-3-inch loaf pan with cooking spray.

2. In a large bowl, mix together the flour, baking powder, baking soda, cinnamon, sugar, and salt.

3. Add the vanilla, water, and bananas to the bowl and stir until just combined.

4. Stir half the walnuts into the batter.

5. Pour the batter into the loaf pan and smooth the top with a spatula.

continued >

Banana Nut Bread, continued

6. Crumple up 4 sheets of aluminum foil into balls and place them in the bottom of the slow cooker. Gently place the filled loaf pan on top of the aluminum foil so that the bottom of the pan is not resting directly on the bottom of the crock insert.

7. Sprinkle with the remaining walnuts.

8. Cook on high for 2 to 3 hours, leaving the lid propped open with a wooden spoon. The bread is done when a knife inserted in the center comes out clean.

9. Remove the bread from the slow cooker and let it cool for 5 minutes in the loaf pan. Then run a knife around the edges of the bread and carefully invert it onto a rack to cool completely, about 1 hour.

Rich and Hearty Black Bread

SERVES 6 | **COOK TIME** 1½ HOURS | **HIGH**

This rich, slightly sweet, earthy-flavored, and seductively dark-hued bread is based on a traditional Russian recipe. Its dark color comes from the addition of molasses, coffee, and cocoa. Its flavor is so rich that it needs nothing more than a slather of butter, but it's also fantastic topped with a layer of melted cheese or toasted and dunked into a bowl of soup.

Cooking spray

Parchment paper

1 cup warm whole milk

1 tablespoon rapid rise yeast

1 tablespoon granulated sugar

1 teaspoon salt

2 teaspoons molasses

4 tablespoons unsalted
    butter, melted

¾ cup honey

1 tablespoon unsweetened
    Dutch-processed cocoa powder

2 tablespoons granulated
    instant coffee

2½ cups unbleached
    all-purpose flour

Per serving: Calories 431; Fat 10g; Protein 8g; Carbohydrates 81g; Fiber 2g; Sodium 463mg

1. Coat the bottom and sides of the slow cooker with cooking spray.

2. Line the bottom with parchment paper and coat it again with cooking spray.

3. In the bowl of a stand mixer fitted with the paddle attachment, mix together the milk, yeast, and sugar. Let the mixture rest for 5 minutes to activate the yeast.

4. Beat in the salt, molasses, butter, and honey.

5. With the machine running, beat in the cocoa powder and instant coffee, and then add the flour ½ cup at a time, beating between additions.

continued >

Rich and Hearty Black Bread, continued

6. Switch to the dough hook attachment and mix the dough until it is smooth and elastic.

7. Allow the dough to rest for 5 minutes.

8. Pull off pieces of dough to form dinner roll–size balls. Layer the dough balls in the slow cooker.

9. Cover and cook on high for 1½ hours or until the bread is firm.

Slow-Baked Yeast Bread

SERVES 6 | **COOK TIME** 1½ TO 2½ HOURS | **HIGH**

This is a great basic bread recipe. The beauty of making yeast bread in the slow cooker is that the low temperature allows the dough to both rise and bake, so you don't have to attend to it for both steps. The best way to test the doneness of the bread is with an instant-read thermometer. A fully baked loaf will have an internal temperature of 190°F to 200°F.

Cooking spray

Parchment paper

1¼ cups warm water, divided

2¼ teaspoons active dry yeast

1 teaspoon granulated sugar

1 egg

¼ cup grapeseed oil (or another neutral-flavored oil, such as safflower or sunflower seed oil)

1 teaspoon salt

3½ to 4 cups unbleached all-purpose flour

Per serving: Calories 363; Fat 11g; Protein 9g; Carbohydrates 57g; Fiber 2g; Sodium 402mg

1. Coat the bottom and sides of the slow cooker with cooking spray.

2. Line the bottom with parchment paper and coat it again with cooking spray.

3. In the bowl of a stand mixer fitted with the paddle attachment, combine ¼ cup of warm water with the yeast and sugar. Let the mixture rest for 5 minutes to activate the yeast.

4. Add the egg, oil, remaining 1 cup of water, and salt to the bowl.

5. With the machine running, add the flour ½ cup at a time, beating between additions.

continued >

Slow-Baked Yeast Bread, continued

6. Switch to the dough hook attachment and mix the dough until it is smooth and elastic.

7. Allow the dough to rest for 5 minutes.

8. Shape the dough into a loaf and place it in the slow cooker.

9. Cover and cook on high for 1½ to 2½ hours, or until the bread is firm and it registers 190°F to 200°F on an instant-read thermometer.

Tip: When it's done, this bread won't be browned on the top. If you love a crusty brown loaf, broil it under low heat for 5 minutes, or just until it browns.

Overnight Cinnamon Buns

SERVES 6 | **COOK TIME** 1 HOUR | **HIGH**

These sweet rolls rise overnight (in the slow cooker) and then take only about an hour to cook in the morning. Prep the dough the night before, turn on the slow cooker when you wake up, and you'll have fresh cinnamon buns by the time you're ready to leave for work.

FOR THE BUNS

Cooking spray

Parchment paper

1¼ cups warm water, divided

2¼ teaspoons active dry yeast

1 teaspoon granulated sugar

1 egg

¼ cup grapeseed oil (or another neutral-flavored oil, such as safflower or sunflower seed oil)

1 teaspoon salt

2 tablespoons ground cinnamon

3½ to 4 cups unbleached all-purpose flour

FOR THE ICING

¼ cup confectioners' sugar

Per serving: Calories 426; Fat 11g; Protein 10g; Carbohydrates 72g; Fiber 4g, Sodium 402mg

TO MAKE THE BUNS

1. Coat the bottom and sides of the slow cooker with cooking spray.

2. Line the bottom with parchment paper and coat it again with cooking spray.

3. In the bowl of a stand mixer fitted with the paddle attachment, combine ¼ cup of warm water with the yeast and sugar. Let rest for 5 minutes to activate the yeast.

4. Add the egg, oil, remaining 1 cup of warm water, and salt to the bowl and beat to combine.

5. With the machine running, beat in the cinnamon and then add the flour ½ cup at a time, beating between additions.

continued ›

6. Switch to the dough hook attachment and mix the dough until it is smooth and elastic.

7. Allow the dough to rest for 5 minutes.

8. Shape the dough into six rolls and place them in the slow cooker insert in a single layer.

9. Cover the insert and let it sit overnight at room temperature.

10. The next day, set the slow cooker insert inside the heating element and cook the rolls on high for 1 hour or until they are puffed and firm. Let cool for 20 minutes.

TO MAKE THE ICING

In a small bowl, mix together the confectioners' sugar and 1 teaspoon of cold water. (Use more or less water as needed to make a paste.) Spread the icing on the cooled buns.

Tip: For variety, add chopped pecans to the dough or a bit of grated orange zest to the frosting.

Heartwarming Fruit Compote

SERVES 6 | **COOK TIME** 8 HOURS | **LOW**

If you made *Creamy Overnight Steel-Cut Oats* (page 42) yesterday, then top the leftovers with this sweet and colorful fruit compote. It's also an ideal topping for French toast, waffles, or pancakes. Feel free to add any fruits you like. This doesn't freeze very well, but it will keep for about a week in the refrigerator.

Cooking spray

½ **cup granulated sugar**

½ **cup water**

½ **teaspoon pure vanilla extract**

¼ **cup pitted and halved fresh cherries**

¼ **cup hulled and halved strawberries**

¼ **cup cubed pineapple**

1 **orange, peeled and sliced**

¼ **cup pitted prunes**

¼ **cup raisins (golden or dark)**

¼ **cup dried apricots**

¼ **cup sliced peaches (fresh, or frozen and thawed)**

1. Coat the slow cooker with cooking spray.

2. In the slow cooker, stir together all the ingredients.

3. Cook on low for 8 hours.

Tip: You can completely customize this to the season. Add diced pumpkin and sweet potato in the fall or fresh berries in the summer. Watermelon tends to fall apart, so avoid using it in this recipe.

Per serving: Calories 137; Fat 0g; Protein 11g; Carbohydrates 36g; Fiber 3g; Sodium 2mg

4

Sizeable Sides

Zesty Orange-Cranberry Sauce

SERVES 6 | **COOK TIME** 8 HOURS | **LOW**

Classically flavored with sugar and orange zest, this is the easiest cranberry sauce recipe you will ever make. The cranberries "pop" and thicken this sauce naturally. Play around with the amount of sugar, as some people like it sweeter than others. Serve the sauce warm or chilled.

5 cups fresh cranberries, washed

1 cup granulated sugar

2 cups orange juice

1 tablespoon freshly grated orange zest

½ teaspoon salt

Per serving: Calories 213; Fat 0g; Protein 1g; Carbohydrates 51g; Fiber 4g; Sodium 194mg

1. In the slow cooker, combine all the ingredients.

2. Cook on low for 8 hours.

Tip: *To zest an orange, rub a clean, unpeeled orange against the finest side of a box or hand grater, stopping just before you hit the bitter white pith of the orange. Use the rest of the orange for juice, or cut it into wedges for a chef's snack.*

Madras Curried Lentils

SERVES 4 | **COOK TIME** 8 HOURS | **LOW**

Lentils are a staple of Indian cooking. They're inexpensive, versatile, nutritious, and easy to make. Here they're simmered with tomato purée, coconut milk, and Indian spices for a flavorful and satisfying meal.

2 cups dried lentils

1½ cups tomato purée

1 (5.5-ounce) can tomato paste

½ large yellow onion, finely diced

1 large potato, peeled and cubed

1 (14-ounce) can unsweetened coconut milk

3 garlic cloves, minced

1 teaspoon turmeric

½ teaspoon ground coriander

1 teaspoon curry powder

1 teaspoon ground cumin

½ teaspoon salt

Per serving: Calories 724; Fat 25g; Protein 33g; Carbohydrates 98g; Fiber 39g; Sodium 538mg

1. In the slow cooker, mix all the ingredients.

2. Cook on low for 8 hours.

Tip: *Lentils are marketed in four general categories: brown, green, red and yellow, and specialty. In general, the brown and green varieties retain their shape well (some more fully than others), whereas the split red and yellow lentils tend to disintegrate and are best for soups or in recipes where they'll be puréed.*

Jack's Bourbon-Mango BBQ Beans

SERVES 16 | **COOK TIME** 8 HOURS | **LOW**

A shot of bourbon and a bit of diced chipotle chile take these sweet, spicy baked beans over the top. Bring them to your next potluck to ensure that you'll have one delicious vegetarian item to eat—if you can keep the omnivores from eating it all, that is. You can heat up the leftovers for topping baked potatoes or leave them cold and toss them into a salad.

Cooking spray

2 (16-ounce) bags dried navy beans, soaked overnight and drained

1 large sweet onion (such as Vidalia), chopped

1 mango, peeled and diced

1½ cups Best Barbecue Sauce (see page 193)

1¼ cups water

2 tablespoons balsamic vinegar

1 teaspoon honey

1 ounce bourbon

½ chipotle pepper, chopped (or to taste)

¼ teaspoon salt (optional)

1. Coat the slow cooker with cooking spray.

2. In the slow cooker, stir together all the ingredients.

3. Cook on low for 8 hours.

Tip: You can use different kinds of beans here. Black or pinto beans would also work well.

Per serving: Calories 255; Fat 1g; Protein 13g; Carbohydrates 49g; Fiber 14g; Sodium 377mg

Triple Mushroom Rice

SERVES 8 | **COOK TIME** 8 HOURS | **LOW**

This recipe calls for three kinds of mushrooms and two kinds of rice. Feel free to substitute other varieties of mushrooms if you like. If you're not vegan, top the dish with a bit of grated Parmesan cheese.

Cooking spray

1 (16-ounce) bag uncooked long-grain rice

½ cup uncooked wild rice

4 ounces white mushrooms, sliced

4 ounces baby portobello mushrooms, sliced

4 ounces cremini mushrooms, sliced

3 cups Vegetable Broth (page 26), or store-bought

Salt

1. Coat the slow cooker with cooking spray.

2. In the slow cooker, stir together all the ingredients, except rice.

3. Cook on low for 8 hours, and season with salt before serving.

Tip: *For variety, stir in some slivered almonds just before serving. Or try raisins, dried cranberries, or other dried fruits.*

Per serving: Calories 267; Fat 1g; Protein 9g; Carbohydrates 55g; Fiber 2g; Sodium 291mg

Vegetable Tikka Masala

SERVES 6 | **COOK TIME** 8 HOURS AND 15 MINUTES | **LOW**

There are many slow cooker recipes for the Indian staple Tikka Masala, but most require lots of prep time. This recipe requires no more than ten minutes of slicing and chopping and tastes truly authentic. Be sure to add the cream or yogurt during the last hour of cooking so it doesn't curdle.

2 carrots, peeled and sliced

1 onion, chopped

1 large tomato, chopped

1 cup sliced mushrooms

4 garlic cloves, finely minced

3 tablespoons minced fresh ginger

1 (29-ounce) can tomato purée

2 tablespoons garam masala

2 teaspoons ground turmeric

2 teaspoons ground cumin

½ teaspoon paprika

¼ teaspoon salt

½ teaspoon ground cinnamon

½ teaspoon cayenne pepper
   (more or less depending
   on taste)

1 cup heavy cream or plain yogurt

3 tablespoons cornstarch

1. In the slow cooker, stir together all the ingredients except the cream and cornstarch. Cook on low for 8 hours.

2. In a small bowl, whisk together the cream and cornstarch and stir the mixture into the vegetables in the slow cooker. Turn the heat to high and cook, uncovered, for 15 more minutes.

Tip: You can also add some tofu or some softer vegetables like spinach or zucchini when you add the cream and cornstarch.

Per serving: Calories 179; Fat 8g; Protein 4g; Carbohydrates 26g; Fiber 5g; Sodium 167mg

Bread Stuffing with Mushrooms and Herbs

SERVES 6 | **COOK TIME** 6 TO 8 HOURS | **LOW**

Using your slow cooker to make stuffing is a brilliant way to free up your oven for other things when cooking a festive holiday meal. This recipe produces a classic flavorful stuffing that stays extra moist since the slow cooker seals in all the tasty broth and other juices. The key to success in this recipe is to use toasted bread cubes so they don't get mushy. Also, start checking the stuffing after 6 hours so it doesn't get overcooked.

Cooking spray

Parchment paper

2 onions, chopped

2 celery stalks, chopped

1 (12-ounce) package sliced
  mushrooms

12 cups toasted bread cubes

1 tablespoon poultry seasoning

½ teaspoon salt

1 tablespoon chopped fresh sage

1 teaspoon chopped fresh thyme

3 ½ cups Vegetable Broth
  (page 26), or store-bought

Per serving: Calories 427; Fat 7g; Protein 25g; Carbohydrates 69g; Fiber 12g; Sodium 1,362mg

1. Coat the slow cooker with cooking spray.

2. Line the bottom with parchment paper and coat it again with cooking spray.

3. In a very large bowl, toss together all the ingredients. Transfer the mixture to the slow cooker, and cook for 6 to 8 hours on low.

Tip: Fresh herbs are much more flavorful than their dried counterparts, but if you can't find fresh, substitute 1 teaspoon dried sage and ¼ teaspoon dried thyme.

German Potato Salad

SERVES 6 | **COOK TIME** 6 TO 8 HOURS | **LOW**

Classic German potato salad is served warm with bacon and vinegar dressing. This vegetarian recipe for warm potato salad leaves out the bacon (although you can add vegetarian bacon bits if you wish), but maintains the delicious vinegary flavor. Though russet potatoes are the traditional choice, here we use new red potatoes instead because they hold their shape better in the slow cooker.

Cooking spray

6 cups quartered new
   red potatoes

1 teaspoon salt

¼ teaspoon freshly ground
   black pepper

1 tablespoon chopped
   fresh thyme

2 tablespoons granulated sugar

¼ cup water

½ red onion, thinly sliced

2 celery stalks, thinly sliced

2 tablespoons chopped
   fresh dill

2 tablespoons chopped
   fresh chives

¼ cup apple cider vinegar

¼ cup olive oil

2 tablespoons Dijon mustard

1. Coat the slow cooker with cooking spray.

2. In the slow cooker, stir together the potatoes, salt, pepper, thyme, sugar, and water.

3. Cook on low for 6 to 8 hours or until the potatoes are fork tender.

Tip: If you're using vegetarian bacon bits, add them along with the parsley.

Per serving: Calories 207; Fat 9g; Protein 4g; Carbohydrates 30g; Fiber 3g; Sodium 464mg

Indian Red Bean Curry

SERVES 6 | **COOK TIME** 8 HOURS | **LOW**

This rustic red bean curry, flavored with garam masala and fresh ginger, is a dinner-table staple throughout India. It is traditionally served over rice, but it's also perfect over other grains like quinoa or bulgur or with a side of chewy Indian flatbread (naan) for scooping. Although the classic recipe uses kidney beans, this one uses pinto beans because they are a bit sturdier and will hold up better to the long cooking time.

3 cups dried pinto beans,
    soaked overnight

1 medium onion,
    roughly chopped

2 medium tomatoes, diced

2 tablespoons chopped
    fresh ginger

3 garlic cloves, chopped

¼ teaspoon ground cloves

½ teaspoon ground cinnamon

1 tablespoon whole cumin seeds

1 tablespoon cayenne pepper
    (or to taste)

1 teaspoon garam masala

4 cups water

½ cup chopped fresh cilantro

1 teaspoon salt

––––––––––

Per serving: Calories 366; Fat 2g; Protein 22g; Carbohydrates 67g; Fiber 17g; Sodium 411mg

1. In the slow cooker, stir together all the ingredients except the cilantro and salt.

2. Cook on low for 8 hours. Just before serving, stir in the cilantro and salt.

Tuscan White Beans with Sun-Dried Tomatoes

SERVES 6 | **COOK TIME** 8 HOURS AND 15 MINUTES | **LOW**

This Tuscan-inspired dish is packed with flavor and nutrition. Sun-dried tomatoes, Kalamata olives, and fresh basil add bright, intense flavor to the otherwise mild and creamy beans. Serve these beans on their own as a main dish, or spoon them over toasted slices of rustic French bread for a quick appetizer.

1 pound dried white beans, soaked overnight

2 garlic cloves, finely chopped

6 cups water

1 tablespoon chopped fresh basil

1 teaspoon salt

¼ teaspoon freshly ground black pepper

1 cup sliced sun-dried tomatoes packed in oil

¼ cup pitted Kalamata olives, sliced

1. In the slow cooker, add the beans, garlic, and water. Cook on low for 8 hours or until the beans are tender.

2. Add the basil, salt, pepper, tomatoes, and olives, turn the slow cooker to high, and cook for 15 more minutes.

Tip: You can use any type of olive or add capers, lemon slices, artichoke hearts, or other Mediterranean ingredients.

Per serving: Calories 323; Fat 1g; Protein 19g; Carbohydrates 49g; Fiber 15g; Sodium 833mg

Spinach Artichoke Dip

SERVES 12 | **COOK TIME** 4 HOURS | **LOW**

This classic dip is always a popular party dish. This recipe makes enough for a crowd, and better yet, it can be kept in the slow cooker on the warm setting throughout the party. Serve it with slices of crusty bread or crackers for dipping.

Cooking spray

1 (10-ounce) bag fresh baby spinach, roughly chopped

1 (14-ounce) can artichoke hearts, drained and chopped

½ cup sour cream

½ cup mayonnaise

½ cup diced yellow onion

1 garlic clove, finely minced

1 cup shredded mozzarella cheese

¼ cup grated Parmesan cheese

¼ cup whole milk

1 (8-ounce) package cream cheese, cubed

Per serving: Calories 208; Fat 16g; Protein 10g; Carbohydrates 9g; Fiber 2g; Sodium 327mg

1. Coat the slow cooker with cooking spray.

2. In the slow cooker, stir together the spinach, artichokes, sour cream, mayonnaise, onion, garlic, mozzarella, Parmesan, milk, and cream cheese.

3. Cook on low for 4 hours.

Tip: For a twist, substitute half the spinach with chopped kale, or stir in some chopped tomatoes just before serving.

Cilantro and Lime Rice

SERVES 6 | **COOK TIME** 8 HOURS | **LOW**

Rice made with cilantro and lime has become a mainstream favorite of Mexican food lovers in recent years. The rice cooks until it is moist and fluffy before the lime zest, lime juice, and cilantro are stirred in. You could make a big batch of this recipe and refrigerate it for use in burritos, tacos, and numerous other dishes all week long. And who says you can't mix cuisines? This rice paired with *Indian Red Bean Curry* (page 70) takes two sides and makes one complete, and completely flavorful, meal.

3 cups water

2 tablespoons unsalted butter

1 teaspoon sea salt

1½ cups uncooked long-grain converted white rice (not instant)

2 teaspoons lime zest

3 teaspoons fresh lime juice

¾ cup chopped fresh cilantro, plus ¼ cup for garnish

1. Mix the water, butter, salt, and rice in the slow cooker.

2. Cook on low for 4 hours.

3. Stir in the lime zest, lime juice, and ¾ cup of cilantro.

4. Top with the remaining cilantro and serve.

Per serving: Calories 204; Fat 4g; Protein 3g; Carbohydrates 37g; Fiber 1g; Sodium 347mg

5
Soups

Healing Vegetable Soup

SERVES 8 | **COOK TIME** 8 HOURS | **LOW**

This simple soup is loaded with vitamin-rich vegetables, making it the perfect dish to slurp whenever you're feeling under the weather. Make a double batch and stash some in the freezer so you have some on hand whenever you feel a cold coming on.

1 large onion, chopped

2 large carrots, peeled and sliced

2 large celery stalks, sliced

2 zucchini, chopped

5 garlic cloves, smashed

8 cups Vegetable Broth (page 26)

2 bay leaves

2 teaspoons sea salt

½ teaspoon freshly ground black pepper

2 tablespoons chopped fresh basil

1 cup grated Parmesan cheese (optional)

1. In the slow cooker, stir together all the ingredients except the basil and the cheese, if using.

2. Cook on low for 8 hours.

3. Remove the bay leaves. Stir in the basil and serve garnished with the Parmesan cheese.

Tip: If you're freezing some, first let it cool completely, then transfer it to an airtight container. It will keep in the freezer for several months.

Per serving: Calories 310; Fat 7g; Protein 25g; Carbohydrates 40g; Fiber 10g; Sodium 1,285mg

Corn and Red Pepper Chowder

SERVES 6 | **COOK TIME** 8 HOURS AND 15 MINUTES | **LOW**

This soup is fantastic in the summer made with corn fresh from the cob and peppers from your garden or the farmers' market. In the winter, it's fine to use frozen (thawed) or canned corn and red peppers from the supermarket.

4 cups corn kernels

1 medium onion, diced

1 medium bell pepper, diced

3 cups quartered new red potatoes

4 cups Vegetable Broth (page 26), or store-bought

1 teaspoon ground cumin

⅛ teaspoon cayenne pepper (or to taste)

½ teaspoon smoked paprika

¼ teaspoon salt (optional)

1 cup unsweetened almond milk

_____

Per serving: Calories 222; Fat 1g; Protein 6g; Carbohydrates 50g; Fiber 5g; Sodium 390mg

1. In the slow cooker, stir together all the ingredients except the almond milk.

2. Cook on low for 8 hours.

3. Add the almond milk, and cook on low for 15 more minutes.

4. Turn off the heat and allow the soup to cool slightly.

5. Using an immersion blender, purée the soup to the desired level of chunkiness.

Tip: If you don't have an immersion blender, you can use a regular blender. Just work in small batches and cover the lid of the blender with a towel in case it spatters.

Hot and Sour Soup

SERVES 8 | **COOK TIME** 8 HOURS AND 15 MINUTES | **LOW**

Hot and sour soup is a classic Szechuan dish that gets a hit of acid from vinegar and a kick of heat from white pepper, both stirred in just before serving for maximum flavor. Vegan versions are hard to come by, but this one is sure to satisfy. Adjust the amount of vinegar and pepper to your taste, and add diced tofu or beaten egg (if you're not vegan) for added protein.

1 (10-ounce) package sliced mushrooms

8 fresh shiitake mushrooms, stems discarded, caps sliced

1 (8-ounce) can bamboo shoots, drained and cut into matchstick pieces

4 garlic cloves, minced

2 tablespoons grated fresh ginger

4 cups water

2 tablespoons vegan chicken-flavored bouillon

2 tablespoons soy sauce

1 teaspoon sesame oil

1 teaspoon chili paste

1½ cups fresh or frozen (and thawed) peas

2 tablespoons rice wine vinegar or apple cider vinegar

1 teaspoon white pepper

1. In the slow cooker, stir together all the ingredients except the peas, vinegar, and pepper.

2. Cook on low for 8 hours.

3. Add the peas to the slow cooker and cook on low for 15 more minutes.

4. Just before serving, stir in the vinegar and pepper.

Tip: *For a gluten-free version, substitute gluten-free soy sauce.*

Per serving: Calories 102; Fat 2g; Protein 6g; Carbohydrates 19g; Fiber 4g; Sodium 447mg

Italian Minestrone

SERVES 6 | **COOK TIME** 8 HOURS AND 15 MINUTES | **LOW**

Minestrone means "big soup," and this Italian classic—filled with pasta, beans, and veggies—always delivers. Traditionally it's made with kidney beans, but we use cooked white beans here because they will hold their shape better. Serve this soup with crusty Italian bread.

1 cup cooked white beans (page 25)

6 cups Vegetable Broth (page 26), or store-bought

½ cup chopped onion

1 cup diced carrots

½ cup diced celery

2 garlic cloves, minced

1 (28-oz) can diced tomatoes with their juices

1 sprig fresh rosemary

2 bay leaves

2 tablespoons chopped fresh basil

¼ cup chopped fresh flat-leaf parsley

½ teaspoon kosher salt

Freshly ground black pepper to taste

4 cups chopped fresh spinach

2 cups cooked small pasta

1. In the slow cooker, stir together all the ingredients except the spinach and pasta.

2. Cook on low for 8 hours.

3. Add the spinach and pasta to the slow cooker and cook on low for 15 more minutes.

Tip: It's a good idea to keep some cooked pasta in the freezer for use in slow cooker recipes.

Per serving: Calories 351; Fat 2g; Protein 17g; Carbohydrates 66g; Fiber 9g; Sodium 913mg

Pasta Fagioli

SERVES 6 | **COOK TIME** 8 HOURS AND 15 MINUTES | **LOW**

Pasta Fagioli means "pasta beans," and it is a classic Italian peasant dish that combines inexpensive and hearty ingredients like beans and veggies into a richly satisfying tomato-based soup. Unlike the kind you'll find in most Italian restaurants, this one's vegan. If you're not a vegan, you can add the rind of some Parmesan cheese to the slow cooker at the beginning of cooking. It adds a wonderful depth to the flavor.

1 onion, chopped

3 carrots, peeled and chopped

4 celery stalks, chopped

2 (28-ounce) cans diced tomatoes with their juices

2 cups kidney beans, cooked (see page 25)

2 cups white kidney beans, cooked (see page 25)

1 quart Vegetable Broth (page 26), or store-bought

1 tablespoon dried oregano

1 bay leaf

2 teaspoons freshly ground black pepper

3 cups Simmered Marinara Sauce (page 27), or store-bought

2 cups cooked tiny pasta shapes

1. In the slow cooker, stir together all the ingredients except the pasta.

2. Cook on low for 8 hours.

3. Add the pasta and cook on low for 15 more minutes, seasoning with salt before serving.

Tip: Dried oregano works better here than fresh, so no need to go out of your way to get the fresh stuff.

Per serving: Calories 666; Fat 5g; Protein 36g; Carbohydrates 123g; Fiber 33g; Sodium 1,353mg

Smoky Split Pea Soup

SERVES 6 | **COOK TIME** 8 HOURS | **LOW**

Traditional split pea soup is made with a ham hock and diced ham to give it a smoky flavor. This meat-free version uses liquid smoke instead. If you like a kick of heat, add a dash of cayenne pepper to taste. This is one of those recipes where you'll need to know your slow cooker, as it might take more than 8 hours for the peas to soften to the consistency you like.

2 ½ cups dried green split peas

3 shallots, chopped

3 to 4 celery stalks, chopped

2 small carrots, peeled and chopped

6 cups Vegetable Broth (page 26), or store-bought

1 teaspoon curry powder (optional)

Leaves from 2 sprigs fresh thyme

2 to 3 drops liquid smoke

Salt

Per serving: Calories 314; Fat 1g; Protein 21g; Carbohydrates 57g; Fiber 23g; Sodium 562mg

1. In the slow cooker, stir together all the ingredients.

2. Cook for 8 hours, or until the peas are tender.

3. If desired, use an immersion blender or regular blender to purée the soup. Season with salt before serving.

Tip: Liquid smoke is created by burning wood chips and then condensing the smoke into a liquid. It's very concentrated, so only use a few drops. Liquid smoke is a vegetarian's best friend, as it's an ideal way to get a smoky flavor without meat.

Creamy Broccoli and Blue Cheese Soup

SERVES 6 | **COOK TIME** 4 HOURS | **LOW**

This recipe cooks in less time than the typical slow cooker recipe. This is because broccoli will disintegrate if it cooks for too long. If you prefer softer broccoli, start with frozen broccoli that's been defrosted. You can use any type of blue cheese here as long as it is creamy. Gorgonzola, Stilton, or Roquefort are all fine choices.

2 tablespoons butter

6 scallions, chopped

¼ cup unbleached all-purpose flour

1 (12-ounce) can evaporated milk

1 teaspoon dried thyme

4 cups broccoli florets

4 cups Vegetable Broth (page 26), or store-bought

12 ounces crumbled blue cheese

½ teaspoon freshly ground black pepper

1 fresh red chile pepper, seeded and chopped

1. In the slow cooker, stir together all the ingredients.

2. Cook on low for 4 hours.

3. Before serving, purée the soup in batches in a countertop blender or using an immersion blender.

Per serving: Calories 383; Fat 26g; Protein 22g; Carbohydrates 17g; Fiber 2g; Sodium 1,453mg

Caribbean-Style Black Bean Soup

SERVES 6 | **COOK TIME** 8 HOURS | **LOW**

Black bean soup—black beans simmered for hours with warming spices and vegetables—is a hallmark of Caribbean cuisine. Cooking the soup in the slow cooker gives it the time it needs to develop and meld the deep flavors of the ingredients. Top it with a dollop of sour cream or crème fraîche or, if you're vegan, a drizzle of *Garlic Cashew Cream Sauce* (page 185).

2 cups cooked black beans
(see page 25)

1 (14.5-ounce) can diced
tomatoes, drained

2 garlic cloves, chopped

1 red bell pepper, diced

1 teaspoon ground cinnamon

1 teaspoon ground allspice

1 tablespoon ground cumin

1 teaspoon chipotle chili powder

Juice of 1 orange

Juice of 1 lime

4 cups Vegetable Broth
(page 26), or store-bought

Salt

1. In the slow cooker, stir together all the ingredients.

2. Cook on low for 8 hours.

3. If you want a smoother soup, purée it with an immersion blender or in a regular blender. Season with salt before serving.

Per serving: Calories 283; Fat 2g; Protein 19g; Carbohydrates 49g; Fiber 12g; Sodium 523mg

Simple Tomato Soup with Fresh Basil

SERVES 6 | **COOK TIME** 8 HOURS | **LOW**

Few things are more comforting than a big bowl of tomato soup. This version requires hardly more of your time than it would take to open and heat up a can, but the result is much more satisfying, not to mention healthier. To make it a bit heartier, you can add cooked rice or pasta after puréeing the soup. Let it cook for an additional 15 minutes to heat through.

3 large carrots, peeled and roughly chopped

2 celery stalks, diced

2 medium sweet onions, roughly chopped

4 garlic cloves, chopped

2 teaspoons salt

¼ teaspoon freshly ground black pepper

5 large tomatoes, peeled and chopped

6 cups Vegetable Broth (page 26), or store-bought

¼ cup chopped fresh basil

Per serving: Calories 99; Fat 2g; Protein 7g; Carbohydrates 15g; Fiber 4g; Sodium 1,577mg

1. In the slow cooker, stir together all the ingredients except the basil.

2. Cook on low for 8 hours.

3. Turn off the slow cooker and let the soup cool slightly.

4. With an immersion blender or in a regular blender, purée the soup until smooth.

5. Just before serving, stir in the basil.

Tip: To easily remove the skin from a tomato, cut an X in the bottom of the tomato using a sharp knife, then blanch it in boiling water for one minute. Using tongs, remove the tomato from the water and let it cool. Once it has cooled, the skin should slip right off.

Potato and Leek Soup with Cheddar Cheese

SERVES 6 | **COOK TIME** 8 HOURS AND 15 MINUTES | **LOW**

This classic soup is always in style because it is the ultimate in comfort food—simple, hearty, and delicious. Potatoes and leeks are simmered in broth and then enriched with sharp cheese and rich cream. Serve it as is or top with your favorite baked potato toppings such as vegetarian bacon bits, chopped chives or scallions, or additional shredded cheese.

5 medium russet potatoes, peeled and diced

6 cups Vegetable Broth (page 26), or store-bought

2 medium leeks, white and pale green parts only, halved and thinly sliced

4 garlic cloves, minced

¼ cup shredded Cheddar cheese

2 tablespoons unsalted butter

1 teaspoon salt

¼ cup heavy cream

Freshly ground black pepper

Per serving: Calories 142; Fat 9g; Protein 7g; Carbohydrates 8g; Fiber 1g; Sodium 1,650mg

1. In the slow cooker, stir together the potatoes, broth, leeks, garlic, cheese, butter, and salt.

2. Cook on low for 8 hours.

3. Add the cream and season with black pepper, then cook for 15 more minutes.

4. For a smooth soup, purée using an immersion blender or in a regular blender.

Tip: *This soup thickens a lot as it cools; add some water to thin it out if needed.*

Flavorful Pho

SERVES 6 | **COOK TIME** 8 HOURS | **LOW**

Pho is a traditional Vietnamese clear-broth beef soup that's loaded up with rice noodles and fresh herbs and veggies. Thanks to the use of vegan "beef" bouillon, this vegan version tastes very much like the original, but without the meat. If you enjoy eating tofu, feel free to add in cubed tofu during the last hour of cooking.

6 cups Vegetable Broth (page 26) or store-bought

2 tablespoons firmly packed light brown sugar

2 cups water

1 packet vegan "beef" bouillon

2 tablespoons crumbled dried seaweed (see Tip)

6 whole cloves

1 (2-inch) piece fresh ginger, peeled and thinly sliced

1 cinnamon stick

6 ounces wide rice noodles

2 cups mung bean sprouts

2 cups fresh basil leaves

1 cup fresh mint leaves

1 cup fresh cilantro leaves

1 fresh Thai or serrano chile, seeded and thinly sliced

1 lime, cut into 6 wedges

Per serving: Calories 114; Fat 2g; Protein 9g; Carbohydrates 17g; Fiber 2g; Sodium 1,056mg

1. In the slow cooker, stir together the broth, brown sugar, water, bouillon, crumbled seaweed, cloves, ginger, and cinnamon stick.

2. Cook for 7 hours and 40 minutes. Add the rice noodles for the last 20 minutes of cooking and fully submerge them before closing the slow cooker.

continued >

Flavorful Pho, continued

3. Just before serving, remove the cinnamon stick. Ladle the broth into serving bowls and top each with bean sprouts, basil, mint, cilantro, chile, and lime.

Tip: Crunchy toasted seaweed can be found in most supermarkets these days. In vegan soups, it adds a briny seafood flavor without the fish. It makes a great substitute for fish sauce in Asian dishes.

Fireside Winter Soup

SOY-FREE
GLUTEN-FREE
NUT-FREE
VEGAN

SERVES 6 | **COOK TIME** 8 HOURS | **LOW**

This is a great soup to make on a snowy day. It uses many ingredients that you likely already have in your fridge, freezer, or pantry, and you can customize it to your taste. In addition to what's in the recipe, you can add an assortment of wild mushrooms, fresh or dried herbs, broccoli or cauliflower, or dark leafy greens like chard or kale.

3 cups **Vegetable Broth (page 26),
  or store-bought**

3 cups **Simmered Marinara Sauce
  (page 27), or store-bought**

2 **carrots, peeled and chopped**

2 **celery stalks, chopped**

1 **onion, diced**

1 **large tomato, chopped**

4 **new red potatoes, quartered**

1 cup **sliced mushrooms**

1 cup **fresh or frozen (thawed)
  green beans**

¼ cup **corn kernels**

2 or 3 **garlic cloves, halved**

2 **bay leaves**

¼ teaspoon **salt (optional)**

1. In the slow cooker, stir together all the ingredients.

2. Cook on low for 8 hours.

Tip: This recipe freezes particularly well. The only issue is that the potatoes might fall apart, but it's delicious anyway.

Per serving: Calories 230; Fat 3g; Protein 9g; Carbohydrates 44g; Fiber 7g; Sodium 974mg

Late Night Lentil Soup

SERVES 6 | **COOK TIME** 8 HOURS | **LOW**

Spiced with curry powder, ground cumin, and fresh ginger, this easy, delicious, and nutritious lentil soup recipe makes a welcome meal to come home to after a long day or a healthy midnight snack. If you're not a fan of sweet potato, you can leave it out. If you like, spice it up with a dash of *Homemade Hot Pepper Sauce* (page 183) or your favorite store-bought hot sauce.

1 large sweet potato, peeled and diced

3 medium carrots, peeled and cut into ½-inch pieces

¾ cup dried yellow or red lentils

1 (4-inch) piece fresh ginger, peeled and finely grated

1 teaspoon curry powder

1 teaspoon ground cumin

Kosher salt

2 garlic cloves, thinly sliced

Juice of ½ lemon

½ cup chopped fresh cilantro

1. In the slow cooker, stir together the sweet potato, carrots, lentils, ginger, curry powder, cumin, salt, and garlic.

2. Cook on low for 8 hours.

3. Before serving, stir in the lemon juice and cilantro.

Per serving: Calories 130; Fat 1g; Protein 7g; Carbohydrates 25g; Fiber 9g; Sodium 63mg

Albondigas-less Soup

SERVES 6 | **COOK TIME** 8 HOURS | **LOW**

Albondigas soup is a traditional Mexican meatball soup that has a chicken broth base. Mexican spices give this version the same flavors, but without the meat. Rice gives the broth a bit of heft, and you can top it with tortilla strips for added crunch. If you're not vegan, go ahead and top it with shredded cheese.

½ cup uncooked short-grain rice

2 cups chopped onion

1 teaspoon ground cumin

¾ teaspoon salt

1½ teaspoons dried oregano

1 cup chopped carrot

1 garlic clove, minced

1 large tomato, peeled, seeded, and chopped (about 1 cup)

4 cups Vegetable Broth (page 26), or store-bought

2 tablespoons chopped fresh mint

2 cups chopped zucchini

¼ teaspoon freshly ground black pepper

¼ cup chopped fresh cilantro

1. In the slow cooker, stir together all the ingredients except the cilantro.

2. Cook on low for 8 hours.

3. Top with the cilantro before serving.

Tip: *It's not hard to make your own vegetarian "meatballs," and there are many great recipes available. If you desire, add some homemade "meatballs" to this soup during the last hour of cooking.*

Per serving: Calories 121; Fat 1g; Protein 6g; Carbohydrates 22g; Fiber 3g; Sodium 821mg

6

Chilies and Stews

Smoky Bean Chili

SERVES 6 | **COOK TIME** 8 HOURS | **LOW**

Most people are skeptical of vegetarian chili, which too often lacks depth and flavor. This recipe solves that problem by including several flavor-boosting condiments—barbecue sauce, marinara sauce, balsamic vinegar, and salsa—along with the usual herbs and spices. The flavors are deepened and intensified by cooking all day in the slow cooker until they meld and the sauce thickens.

Cooking spray

1 small onion, chopped

2 garlic cloves, finely chopped

2 cups beans, soaked overnight
(black, white, or pinto,
whichever is your favorite)

2 sweet potatoes, peeled
and cubed

2 cups corn kernels

12 cherry tomatoes, quartered

1 (14.5-ounce) can no-salt-added
diced tomatoes with their juices

2 tablespoons Best Barbecue
Sauce (page 193)

1 cup Simmered Marinara Sauce
(page 27), or store-bought

1 cup water

2 tablespoons balsamic vinegar

¼ cup Custom-Designed Salsa
(page 189)

¼ cup chopped fresh cilantro

Dash chili powder

Dash ground cumin

2 avocados, pitted and cubed

Cilantro leaves, for garnish

───────────

Per serving: Calories 347; Fat 15g; Protein 8g;
Carbohydrates 51g; Fiber 15g; Sodium 412mg

1. In the slow cooker, stir together all the ingredients except the avocado and cilantro.

2. Cook on low for 8 hours.

3. Add the avocado before serving, and garnish with cilantro.

Tip: If you don't have fresh cilantro on hand, omit it altogether from the recipe. In this recipe, it's okay to add the cilantro alongside the rest of the ingredients, as we don't want the flavor to stand out.

Chipotle Black Bean and Quinoa Chili

SERVES 6 | **COOK TIME** 8 HOURS | **LOW**

Combining two nutrition powerhouses—quinoa and black beans—makes this dish super nutritious. Cooking them with the bold, balanced flavors of bell pepper, chipotle chile, onion, garlic, and chili powder makes a tantalizing meal. Serve with your favorite toppings, like *Great Guacamole* (page 190), *Custom-Designed Salsa* (page 189), diced onions, sour cream, shredded cheese, or sliced scallions.

1 chipotle chile from
  a can, chopped

2 cups dried black beans,
  soaked overnight

¾ cup uncooked quinoa, rinsed
  and picked over

1 (28-ounce) can no-salt-added
  diced tomatoes with their juices

1 red onion, diced

3 garlic cloves, minced

1 green bell pepper, chopped

1 red bell pepper, chopped

1 cinnamon stick

2 teaspoons chili powder

1 teaspoon ground coriander

¼ cup chopped fresh cilantro

7 cups water

1 teaspoon sea salt

Per serving: Calories 347; Fat 3g; Protein 19g; Carbohydrates 64g; Fiber 15g; Sodium 383mg

1. In the slow cooker, stir together all the ingredients except the salt.

2. Cook on low for 8 hours, or until the beans are soft.

3. Add the salt, remove the cinnamon stick, and serve.

Tip: If you wish, you can add some soy chorizo in the last hour of cooking. If you plan to do so, omit the chili powder, ground coriander, and salt.

Tres Frijoles Chili

SERVES 6 | **COOK TIME** 8 HOURS | **LOW**

Tres frijoles means "three beans" in Spanish. The combination of three different beans gives this chili a unique texture and flavor. We've avoided using black beans here because they tend to make the whole pot of chili turn black. But, if you don't mind that, you can substitute black beans for one of the other types.

2 red bell peppers, diced

1 onion, chopped

2 teaspoons ground cumin

1 teaspoon crushed red pepper flakes

1 teaspoon paprika

1 tablespoon chili powder

4 garlic cloves, thinly sliced

2 cups Vegetable Broth (page 26), or store-bought

1 cup water

1 (28-ounce) can no-salt-added diced tomatoes with their juices

1 cup dried pinto beans, soaked overnight

1 cup dried white beans, soaked overnight

1 cup dried chickpeas, soaked overnight

1 teaspoon salt

1. In the slow cooker, stir together all the ingredients except the salt.

2. Cook on low for 8 hours, or until the beans are soft.

3. Stir in the salt just before serving.

Tip: *This chili freezes very well. When reheating it, the water might separate a bit. Just stir it back in.*

Per serving: Calories 413; Fat 4g; Protein 25g; Carbohydrates 72g; Fiber 20g; Sodium 682mg

Parmesan and White Bean Chili

SERVES 6 | **COOK TIME** 8 HOURS AND 15 MINUTES | **LOW**

White chili is a great alternative to the more common red chili. Traditionally, it's made with chicken, but this vegetarian version is so delicious you won't miss it. The Parmesan cheese, while an unexpected addition to chili, adds a distinctive layer of umami flavor.

3 cups dried white beans, soaked overnight

1½ teaspoons dried oregano

1 teaspoon ground cumin

¼ teaspoon white pepper

2 tablespoons olive oil

1 small yellow onion, chopped

4 garlic cloves, minced

3 tablespoons nutritional yeast

2½ cups Vegetable Broth (page 26), or store-bought

½ teaspoon salt

½ cup grated Parmesan cheese

6 ounces shredded white Cheddar cheese

1. In the slow cooker, stir together all the ingredients except the salt and cheeses.

2. Cook on low for 8 hours.

3. Stir in the salt and Parmesan cheese and cook on low for 15 more minutes.

4. Top each bowl with 1 ounce of the shredded Cheddar cheese.

Tip: Nutritional yeast is a great source of B vitamins, and it adds a savory flavor to foods. It's available in many mainstream grocery stores and almost every health food store.

Per serving: Calories 626; Fat 22g; Protein 45g; Carbohydrates 67g; Fiber 17g; Sodium 972mg

Root Vegetable Stew

SERVES 6 | **COOK TIME** 8 HOURS | **LOW**

Root vegetables are some of the most nutrient-dense foods around. When slow cooked, they develop a deep, sweet, earthy flavor that makes a satisfying stew. Several different root vegetables are combined here—potatoes, carrots, parsnips, turnips, and beets—and spiced with warming spices to make a delicious vegan meal. Make sure to cut the vegetables into similar sizes so they cook evenly.

2 medium yellow onions, diced

1 teaspoon Super Seasoning (page 187)

1¼ teaspoons ground ginger

½ teaspoon ground coriander

¼ teaspoon ground cumin

⅛ teaspoon cayenne pepper

Pinch saffron threads

Dash freshly ground black pepper

3 large Yukon gold potatoes, diced

4 medium carrots, peeled and sliced

4 parsnips, peeled and diced

8 baby turnips, peeled

2 large red beets, peeled and cut into wedges

1 cup white mushrooms, cut in half

3 cups Vegetable Broth (page 26), or store-bought

1. In the slow cooker, combine all the ingredients.

2. Cook on low for 8 hours.

Tip: *The red beets will make this stew very dark in color. If you would like a lighter-colored stew, substitute golden beets instead.*

Per serving: Calories 294; Fat 1g; Protein 10g; Carbohydrates 65g; Fiber 12g; Sodium 568mg

It's Too Hot to Cook Stew

SERVES 6 | **COOK TIME** 8 HOURS | **LOW**

This summery stew is the perfect thing to make when you don't want to heat up your kitchen by turning on the stove. With a bounty of summer vegetables—tomatoes, green beans, yellow squash, and zucchini—it captures the flavors of the season and replenishes your body with the nutrients it needs for another day spent frolicking in the sun.

2 large leeks, cleaned, white and pale green parts sliced (about 2 cups)

2 garlic cloves, minced

2 ½ cups Vegetable Broth (page 26), or store-bought

¾ cup canned diced tomatoes, drained

½ pound green beans, trimmed (about 2 cups)

2 teaspoons Super Seasoning (page 187)

1 medium yellow squash, diced (about 1 cup)

1 medium zucchini, diced (about 1 cup)

1. In the slow cooker, stir together the leeks, garlic, broth, tomatoes, green beans, and Super Seasoning.

2. Cook on low for 7 hours.

3. Add the yellow squash and zucchini and cook on low for 1 more hour.

Tip: *This is a recipe that does not freeze well, as the zucchini and summer squash turn to mush after being frozen. Feel free to substitute any vegetables you have on hand. Just remember to put the soft ones in last.*

Per serving: Calories 62; Fat 1g; Protein 4g; Carbohydrates 11g; Fiber 3g; Sodium 334mg

Chickpea and Mushroom Stew

SOY-FREE
GLUTEN-FREE
NUT-FREE
VEGAN

...TES | **LOW**

...classic Middle Eastern dish. ...natoes, and other vegetables are ...ces to make a fragrant and filling ...scous or just in a big bowl by ...gside. It's also great topped with ...r just a squeeze of lemon.

2 cups dried chickpeas, soaked overnight

1 green bell pepper, diced

1 red bell pepper, diced

2 cups quartered mushrooms

1 medium head of cauliflower, cut into bite-size florets

1 (28-ounce) can diced tomatoes with their juices

¼ teaspoon freshly ground black pepper

10 ounces baby spinach

1 cup unsweetened coconut milk

1 teaspoon salt

Per serving: Calories 477; Fat 16g; Protein 22g; Carbohydrates 69g; Fiber 19g; Sodium 729mg

1. In the slow cooker, stir together the oil, onion, potatoes, curry powder, brown sugar, ginger, garlic, cayenne, broth, chickpeas, bell peppers, mushrooms, cauliflower, tomatoes, and black pepper.

continued >

Chickpea and Mushroom Stew, continued

2. Cook for 8 hours.

3. Add the spinach, coconut milk, and salt, and cook on low for 15 more minutes.

Tip: *Sweet potatoes would be great in this recipe, too. Consider swapping half or all of the fingerling potatoes for sweet potatoes.*

Swiss Chard and White Bean Panade

SERVES 6 | **COOK TIME** 8 HOURS | **LOW**

A panade is a hearty casserole made of vegetables—here we've combined Swiss chard and mushrooms—layered with crusty bread and rich cheese. Cannellini beans make this a substantial meal.

Cooking spray

12 ounces toasted
    bread cubes, divided

1 large onion, thinly sliced

2 cloves garlic, minced

2 cups quartered mushrooms

16 ounces Swiss chard, tough
    center ribs removed and leaves
    julienned

1 teaspoon salt

½ teaspoon freshly ground
    black pepper

1½ teaspoons minced fresh thyme
    (or ½ teaspoon dried thyme)

2 (16-ounce) cans cannellini beans

1 cup grated Parmesan cheese,
    divided

6 cups Vegetable Broth (page 26),
    or store-bought

1. Coat the slow cooker with cooking spray and scatter a layer of bread cubes over the bottom.

2. In a large bowl, toss together the onion, garlic, mushrooms, chard, salt, pepper, and thyme.

3. Spread one-third of the vegetable mixture over the bottom of the slow cooker and top with one-third of the beans. Sprinkle ⅓ cup of Parmesan cheese over the beans. Add a second layer of vegetables, beans, and cheese. Top with a layer

continued >

Per serving: Calories 847; Fat 13g; Protein 59g; Carbohydrates 128g; Fiber 41g; Sodium 2,089mg

of vegetables and beans and pour the vegetable broth over the top. Spread the remaining bread cubes in an even layer over the top and finish with the remaining cheese.

4. Cover the slow cooker and cook for 8 hours on low.

Tip: *You can substitute any cooked or canned beans you like for the cannellini beans or substitute another cheese, such as Gruyere, for the Parmesan.*

African Peanut Stew

SERVES 6 | **COOK TIME** 8 HOURS AND 15 MINUTES | **LOW**

This recipe is based on a traditional groundnut stew made with spices, sweet potatoes, and greens common in West Africa. It's a little spicy and a little sweet, and the slow cooker allows the flavors to meld into perfect harmony. Chickpeas are a nontraditional addition, included here for both texture and a boost of protein. You can use either creamy or crunchy peanut butter since you're going to purée it anyway.

3 to 4 garlic cloves, peeled

1 cup loosely packed fresh cilantro leaves and stems

2 inches fresh ginger root, peeled

2 heaping tablespoons peanut butter

1 teaspoon ground cumin

½ teaspoon ground cinnamon

¼ teaspoon cayenne pepper

1 tablespoon curry powder

2 cups dried chickpeas, soaked overnight

2 medium sweet potatoes, peeled and chopped

1 large red bell pepper, chopped

2 cups Vegetable Broth (page 26), or store-bought

1 (14.5-ounce) can diced tomatoes with their juices

½ teaspoon salt

Dash freshly ground black pepper

1½ cups unsweetened coconut milk

1 cup packed baby spinach leaves

_____

Per serving: Calories 545; Fat 22g; Protein 20g; Carbohydrates 72g; Fiber 19g; Sodium 516mg

1. In a food processor or blender, combine the garlic, cilantro, ginger, peanut butter, cumin, cinnamon, cayenne, and curry powder and process until the mixture resembles a thick paste.

2. Add the paste to the slow cooker, along with the chickpeas, sweet potatoes, bell pepper, broth, tomatoes, salt, and black pepper.

3. Cook on low heat for 8 hours.

4. Add the coconut milk and spinach and cook on low for 15 more minutes.

Moroccan Vegetable Stew with Dried Apricots

SERVES 6 | **COOK TIME** 8 HOURS | **LOW**

This hearty vegetable stew is bright with the flavors of North Africa. Don't be intimidated by the long list of ingredients. You probably have most of them already in your pantry. And if you're missing one or two of the spices, it's fine to leave them out—the stew will still be delicious! Serve it over steamed rice, couscous, or quinoa.

1 teaspoon ground cinnamon

1 teaspoon ground cumin

½ teaspoon ground ginger

¼ teaspoon ground cloves

¼ teaspoon ground nutmeg

¼ teaspoon ground turmeric

⅛ teaspoon curry powder

1 tablespoon unsalted butter

1 yellow onion, chopped

2 cups finely shredded kale

4 cups Vegetable Broth (page 26), or store-bought

2 cups dried chickpeas, soaked overnight

1 cup dried lentils, rinsed

1 (14.5-ounce) can diced tomatoes with their juices

3 large Yukon gold potatoes, peeled and diced

2 sweet potatoes, peeled and diced

4 large carrots, peeled and chopped

½ cup chopped dried apricots

1 tablespoon honey

½ teaspoon salt

1 teaspoon freshly ground black pepper

Per serving: Calories 643; Fat 8g; Protein 30g; Carbohydrates 118g; Fiber 30g; Sodium 800mg

1. In the slow cooker, stir together all the ingredients except the salt and pepper.

2. Cook on low for 8 hours.

3. Before serving, stir in the salt and pepper.

Cauliflower and Bean Stew with Jerk Seasoning

SERVES 6 | **COOK TIME** 8 HOURS | **LOW**

This stew is our take on Jerk Chicken—without the chicken. Instead, cauliflower florets and black beans provide the substance and protein. The classic "jerk" spice blend of allspice, red pepper flakes, and other spices along with Scotch bonnet chiles give it a spicy, Jamaican-style kick. Serve this over rice or quinoa, if desired.

2 teaspoons curry powder

1½ teaspoons dried thyme

¾ teaspoon ground allspice

½ teaspoon red pepper flakes

½ teaspoon freshly ground black pepper

1 medium yellow onion, chopped

3 garlic cloves, minced

½ cup dry red wine

1 Scotch bonnet chile, seeded and chopped (see Tip)

1½ cups dried black beans, soaked overnight

1 (14.5-ounce) can diced tomatoes with their juices

1 cup cauliflower florets

½ teaspoon salt

1. In the slow cooker, stir together all the ingredients except the cauliflower and salt.

2. Cook on low for 7 hours.

3. Add the cauliflower and salt and cook on low for 1 more hour.

Tip: Scotch bonnet peppers are extremely hot. Wear gloves when working with them, and don't get them in your nose or eyes! If you like a little less spiciness, you can substitute a milder pepper, like jalapeño.

Per serving: Calories 212; Fat 1g; Protein 12g; Carbohydrates 38g; Fiber 10g; Sodium 207mg

Bountiful Ratatouille

SERVES 8 | **COOK TIME** 8 HOURS | **LOW**

Ratatouille is a classic French stew of summer vegetables—usually tomatoes, eggplant, bell peppers, and summer squash—spiked with garlic and bathed in flavorful olive oil. This slow cooker version is sure to please. You can either peel the eggplant or leave the skin on. Serve with crusty French bread in shallow bowls. Top with freshly grated Parmesan cheese or nutritional yeast.

2 large onions, chopped

1 large eggplant, cut into 2-inch pieces

4 small zucchini, sliced

2 garlic cloves, minced

2 large green bell peppers, chopped

2 large tomatoes, cut into ½-inch-thick wedges

1 (6-ounce) can tomato paste

1 teaspoon dried basil

1 tablespoon chopped fresh oregano

1 teaspoon granulated sugar

2 teaspoons salt

½ teaspoon freshly ground black pepper

2 tablespoons chopped fresh parsley

1 cup Vegetable Broth (page 26)

½ cup dry red wine

_____

Per serving: Calories 100; Fat 1g; Protein 4g; Carbohydrates 20g; Fiber 6g; Sodium 712mg

1. In the slow cooker, stir together all the ingredients.

2. Cook on low for 8 hours.

Tip: When cooking with wine, use a wine that's good enough to drink. Those nasty "cooking wines" are more like vinegar and should be avoided at all costs. This doesn't mean you need to use a $100 bottle of wine, but remember that if it tastes good in your mouth, it will taste good in the stew.

Savory Vegetable Stew with Dumplings

SERVES 6 | **COOK TIME** 8 HOURS | **LOW**

Savory stews topped with dumplings have a long and storied tradition in the South. While normally made with chicken, this version combines hearty potatoes with mushrooms, carrots, green beans, and other vegetables in a stew so flavorful, no one will miss the chicken. The dumpling dough is dolloped on top of the simmering stew where the dumplings cook during the last two hours. While this recipe calls for milk, you can make it vegan by using unflavored nondairy milk instead.

FOR THE STEW

1 onion, finely chopped

2 celery stalks, diced

2 garlic cloves, minced

4 Yukon gold potatoes, diced

3 medium carrots, peeled and diced

½ cup corn kernels

½ cup green beans, trimmed

½ cup quartered white mushrooms

3 cups Vegetable Broth (page 26), or store-bought

3 cups water

Juice of 1 lemon

1 cup Stewed Tomatoes (page 118), or canned

2 bay leaves

Salt

Freshly ground black pepper

½ cup fresh or frozen (and thawed) peas

FOR THE DUMPLINGS

2 cups unbleached all-purpose flour

1½ tablespoons baking powder

¼ teaspoon salt

1½ cups whole milk

1 tablespoon chopped fresh parsley (or 1½ teaspoons dried)

Per serving: Calories 349; Fat 4g; Protein 13g; Carbohydrates 68g; Fiber 6g; Sodium 581mg

continued ›

Savory Vegetable Stew with Dumplings, continued

TO MAKE THE STEW

1. In the slow cooker, stir together the onion, celery, garlic, potatoes, carrots, corn, green beans, mushrooms, broth, water, lemon juice, tomatoes, bay leaves, salt, and pepper.

2. Cook on low for 6 hours.

3. Add the peas to the slow cooker.

TO MAKE THE DUMPLINGS

1. In a small bowl, use a fork to mix together the flour, baking powder, salt, milk, and parsley until it forms a batter.

2. Using an ice cream scoop, arrange scoopfuls of the dumpling batter on top of the stew.

3. Cook on low for 2 more hours, or until the dumplings are cooked through.

Tip: If you have a vegetarian baking mix, you can use that for the dumpling batter instead, following the directions on the box.

een Chile
Potato Stew

...en chiles and sweet potatoes makes for
...Ve've eliminated the sausage usually
...ubstituted white beans. You can add
...f you wish, in the last hour of cooking.

- ...edium Maui onion (or other sweet white onion), chopped
- 3 (4-ounce) cans chopped roasted green chiles, drained
- 4 medium sweet potatoes, diced
- 1 (28-ounce) can diced tomatoes with their juices
- 2 tablespoons tomato paste
- 2 cups water
- 2 cups Vegetable Broth (page 26), or store-bought
- 1 cup dried white beans, soaked overnight
- 1 garlic clove, minced
- ½ teaspoon dried oregano
- ¼ teaspoon freshly ground black pepper
- ¼ teaspoon ground coriander
- 1 teaspoon salt

Per serving: Calories 358; Fat 2g; Protein 16g; Carbohydrates 73g; Fiber 16g; Sodium 1,682mg

1. In the slow cooker, stir together all the ingredients except the salt.

2. Cook on low for 8 hours.

3. Before serving, stir in the salt.

continued >

Roasted Green Chile and Sweet Potato Stew, continued

Tip: If you have the time, substitute the canned green chiles with eight to ten fresh Anaheim chiles, roasted, peeled, and chopped. When you roast them, they add a smoky flavor to all kinds of dishes. To roast them, grease a baking pan with cooking spray and arrange the chiles in a single layer in the prepared pan. Roast at 350°F for about 20 minutes, or until the skins look charred, then remove the chiles from the oven, let them cool slightly, and peel off their skins.

Midsummer Night's Stew

SERVES 4 | **COOK TIME** 6 HOURS | **LOW**

This recipe is reminiscent of a clam bake—without the clams, of course! Corn, potatoes, and mushrooms are simmered in a buttery broth that will make you feel like you're on a beach in New England in the summertime, no matter where or when you eat it. Serve it with crusty bread to sop up the delicious broth.

8 medium new red potatoes

8 ears corn, broken in halves

4 cups halved white mushrooms

½ cup (1 stick) unsalted butter

4 garlic cloves, minced

1 teaspoon sea salt

1 teaspoon freshly ground
    black pepper

3 cups Vegetable Broth (page 26),
    or store-bought

1 cup dry white wine

1 teaspoon red pepper flakes

1. In the slow cooker, combine all the ingredients.

2. Cook on low for 6 hours.

3. To serve, place two potatoes and two halves of corn in each bowl, and ladle the broth on top.

Per serving: Calories 719; Fat 26g; Protein 18g; Carbohydrates 102g; Fiber 12g; Sodium 1,239mg

7

Vegetables

Caramelized Onions

MAKES ABOUT 4 CUPS | **COOK TIME** 8 HOURS | **HIGH**

If you've ever made caramelized onions on the stovetop, you know how high-maintenance they are. With all that stirring and watching, it's almost not worth it. With this recipe, you get all the sweet, oniony goodness without the hassle.

12 medium yellow onions

Cooking spray

¼ cup plus 2 tablespoons olive oil

½ teaspoon kosher salt

Per cup: Calories 312; Fat 21g; Protein 4g; Carbohydrates 31g; Fiber 7g; Sodium 304mg

1. Halve, peel, and slice the onions.

2. Coat the slow cooker with cooking spray.

3. In the slow cooker, toss together the onions, oil, and salt.

4. Cook on high for 8 hours or until the onions are a deep, golden brown.

Tip: This is one of those recipes where it pays to know your slow cooker. Some cookers will take longer than 8 hours—maybe even more than 10 hours—to caramelize this many onions. Others may need less time. Experiment to see what timing works best for you.

Stewed Tomatoes with Fresh Oregano

SERVES 8 | **COOK TIME** 8 HOURS | **LOW**

Many, many recipes call for canned stewed tomatoes. Why buy them when you can make them yourself? This is a great way to use up those tomatoes from the garden. This version is flavored with fresh oregano and would work well in any Italian or Mediterranean dish. Feel free to substitute another fresh herb, such as basil, mint, or cilantro, as desired. Freeze a batch or two and you'll always have stewed tomatoes on hand.

2 pounds tomatoes, peeled and left whole

2 tablespoons granulated sugar

1 teaspoon salt

1 tablespoon fresh oregano

1 garlic clove, finely chopped

2 cups water

1. In the slow cooker, add all of the ingredients.

2. Cook on low for 8 hours.

Tip: To easily peel tomatoes, cut an X in the bottom with a sharp knife and then blanch them in boiling water for 1 minute. The skins should slip off easily. Be careful as they'll be very hot!

Per serving: Calories 34; Fat 0g; Protein 1g; Carbohydrates 8g; Fiber 2g; Sodium 298mg

Vegetarian Gumbo

SERVES 6 | **COOK TIME** 8 HOURS | **LOW**

The quintessential dish of Cajun cooking, gumbo is usually filled with seafood, poultry, and sausage. This vegetarian version may not be very authentic, but it's still delicious. To mimic the richness and depth created by the meat and roux in the traditional version, we use unsweetened cocoa.

1 yellow onion, chopped

1 green bell pepper, chopped

2 celery stalks, chopped

3 garlic cloves, minced

2 tablespoons unbleached all-purpose flour

2 cups Vegetable Broth (page 26), or store-bought

1 (14.5-ounce) can diced tomatoes with their juices

8 ounces white mushrooms, quartered

1 small zucchini, sliced

1 cup frozen sliced okra

2 tablespoons soy sauce

1 tablespoon Cajun seasoning

1 tablespoon unsweetened Dutch-processed cocoa powder

1 bay leaf

Salt

Freshly ground black pepper, to taste

Cooked rice, for serving

Hot pepper sauce, such as Tabasco or Homemade Hot Pepper Sauce (page 183), for serving

---

Per serving: Calories 73; Fat 1g; Protein 6g; Carbohydrates 13g; Fiber 3g; Sodium 658mg

1. In the slow cooker, combine all the ingredients except the rice and hot sauce.

2. Cook on low for 8 hours.

3. Serve over rice and top with the hot sauce.

Tip: Okra can turn a little gummy if it's overcooked. This is why we're using frozen okra instead of fresh.

Decadent Potatoes au Gratin

SERVES 4 | **COOK TIME** 5 TO 7 HOURS | **LOW**

Slow-cooked in cream and layered with cheese, this rich potato dish will make any meal special. Serve it as part of a Thanksgiving spread or with any meal you want people to remember.

Olive oil

3 cups heavy cream

1½ teaspoons salt

¼ teaspoon ground nutmeg

1 teaspoon freshly ground black pepper

3 pounds potatoes, cut into ⅛-inch-thick slices

2 cups grated extra-sharp Cheddar cheese

1 cup freshly grated Parmesan cheese

Per serving: Calories 867; Fat 59g; Protein 31g; Carbohydrates 59g; Fiber 8g; Sodium 1,542mg

1. Coat the slow cooker with oil.

2. In a large bowl, combine the cream, salt, nutmeg, and pepper and stir to combine. Add the potato slices and toss to coat well.

3. In a small bowl, stir the two cheeses together.

4. Arrange one-third of the potatoes in the bottom of the slow cooker. Top with one-third of the cheese. Continue to layer the potatoes and cheese until the ingredients are used up.

5. Pour any remaining cream mixture over the top. Cook on low for 5 to 7 hours.

Black Bean and Spinach Enchiladas

SERVES 4 | **COOK TIME** 3 HOURS | **LOW**

Using premade or store-bought salsa as a sauce makes these enchiladas a cinch to prepare. Filled with a hearty mixture of black beans and spinach and topped with sharp Cheddar cheese, they make a satisfying meal. Serve them topped with sour cream, *Garlic Cashew Cream Sauce* (page 185), *Great Guacamole* (page 190), or more salsa if desired.

1 (15.5-ounce) can black beans, rinsed and drained

1 (10-ounce) package frozen chopped spinach, thawed and squeezed of excess liquid

1 cup frozen corn

½ teaspoon ground cumin

2 cups (about 8 ounces) grated sharp Cheddar cheese, divided

½ teaspoon salt

¼ teaspoon freshly ground black pepper

4 cups salsa, divided

8 (6-inch) corn tortillas, slightly warmed

Sliced scallions, for serving

Per serving: Calories 827; Fat 23g; Protein 48g; Carbohydrates 117g; Fiber 26g; Sodium 2,287mg

1. In a medium bowl, place half of the beans and mash them with a fork.

2. Add the spinach, corn, cumin, 1 cup of cheese, the remaining beans, salt, and pepper to the bowl, and stir to combine.

3. Pour 2 cups of salsa in the bottom of the slow cooker.

4. Place about ½ cup of the filling mixture into each of the tortillas. Roll them up and place them, seam-side down, in a single layer in the slow cooker.

continued >

5. Pour the remaining 2 cups of salsa over the top and sprinkle with the remaining 1 cup of cheese.

6. Cover and cook on low for 3 hours. Serve hot, garnished with the scallions.

Tip: *Replace the black beans with pinto or kidney beans if you wish. You can also replace the Cheddar cheese with Pepper jack cheese for a spicier dish.*

Versatile Yams

SERVES 6 | **COOK TIME** 8 HOURS | **LOW**

This is a simple yam recipe that can be modified in a variety of ways. Once they're cooked, you can mash the yams with some butter, brown sugar, and pecans for a sweet side or toss them with butter and chopped fresh rosemary for a more savory dish. If you're not vegan, add ¼ cup of crumbled feta to the finished dish for an extra kick of flavor.

4 yams, peeled and chopped

1 teaspoon salt

¼ teaspoon freshly ground black pepper

¼ cup water

3 scallions, thinly sliced

6 basil leaves, cut into a chiffonade

Per serving: Calories 141; Fat 3g; Protein 3g; Carbohydrates 27g; Fiber 4g; Sodium 536mg

1. In the slow cooker, combine the yams, salt, pepper, water, and scallions.

2. Cook on low for 8 hours, until the yams are soft.

3. Mix the basil in with the yams before serving.

Tip: Yams are not the same as sweet potatoes. Sweet potatoes are orange inside, whereas yams are white. Some markets sell both, although most just sell sweet potatoes. Either will work equally well in this recipe.

Buttery Southern Carrots, Potatoes, and Corn

SERVES 6 | **COOK TIME** 8 HOURS | **LOW**

This is a delicious side dish that cooks in its own buttery sauce. The key to success is cutting all the vegetables to a similar size (except the corn, of course) so they cook evenly. We've suggested new red potatoes because they hold up particularly well to the long cooking time, but you can use any kind of potato you like.

4 carrots, peeled and cut into coin-size slices

3 cups new red potatoes, washed and sliced

2 cups corn kernels

2 or 3 garlic cloves, minced

½ cup (1 stick) unsalted butter

¼ teaspoon salt

Per serving: Calories 248; Fat 16g; Protein 3g; Carbohydrates 26g; Fiber 4g; Sodium 239mg

1. In the slow cooker, stir together all the ingredients.

2. Cook on low for 8 hours.

Tip: For variety, you can add different spices and herbs, like 1 tablespoon of chopped fresh thyme or a teaspoon or two of Cajun seasoning. You can even add a dash of honey for some sweetness.

Orange-Ginger Glazed Baby Carrots

SERVES 6 | **COOK TIME** 8 HOURS | **LOW**

Cooking carrots in a combination of orange and carrot juices gives them deep flavor. Fresh ginger adds a bright note, while cardamom and garlic add earthy spice. Using baby carrots eliminates most of the prep work for this dish, but if you don't have them, substitute peeled and sliced regular-size carrots.

6 tablespoons unsalted butter

¼ cup peeled and thinly sliced fresh ginger

1 garlic clove, minced

4 cardamom pods

3 pounds baby carrots

2 tablespoons granulated sugar

½ cup fresh carrot juice

½ cup fresh orange juice

Salt

Freshly ground black pepper

1. In the slow cooker, stir together all the ingredients except the salt and pepper.

2. Cook on low for 8 hours.

3. Before serving, season to taste with salt and pepper.

Tip: You can find carrot juice in many grocery stores these days. If you can't find any, it's perfectly fine to use orange juice for the whole thing.

Per serving: Calories 213; Fat 12g; Protein 2g; Carbohydrates 26g; Fiber 7g; Sodium 265mg

Stuffed Tricolor Peppers

SERVES 6 | **COOK TIME** 8 HOURS | **LOW**

In this colorful and healthy dish, peppers are stuffed with the Crazy Simple Quinoa from chapter 2 or plain cooked quinoa, but the recipe is highly adaptable. You could fill them with cooked brown rice, bulgur, farro, beans, or just about anything you can imagine.

Cooking spray

6 bell peppers in assorted colors (2 red, 2 green, and 2 yellow)

3 cups Crazy Simple Quinoa (page 31), or plain cooked quinoa

2 yellow onions, chopped

1 large tomato, chopped

2 cups tightly packed spinach

1 cup chopped mushrooms

2 or 3 garlic cloves, halved

¼ teaspoon salt

Per serving: Calories 359; Fat 5g; Protein 14g; Carbohydrates 64g; Fiber 10g; Sodium 118mg

1. Coat the slow cooker with cooking spray.

2. Cut the tops off the bell peppers and set them aside. Scoop out and discard the seeds and membranes from inside the peppers.

3. In a medium bowl, combine the quinoa, onions, tomato, spinach, mushrooms, garlic, and salt.

4. Arrange the peppers in the slow cooker, cut-sides up. Fill each pepper with ½ cup of the quinoa mixture. Place the tops of the peppers over the filling.

5. Cook on low for 8 hours.

Tip: Reduce the number of peppers if your slow cooker can't accommodate them all. You can keep the leftover quinoa mixture for another recipe.

Asian Garlic Vegetables

SERVES 6 | **COOK TIME** 8 HOURS | **LOW**

Better than takeout, this dish bathes broccoli and other vegetables in a savory sauce flavored with garlic and ginger. Your kitchen will smell amazing! To make this a complete meal, add some cubed extra-firm tofu in the last hour of cooking. Serve over steamed rice, if desired.

1 pound broccoli, leaves removed (stalks left on)

2 carrots, peeled and cut diagonally into ½-inch-thick slices

1 (8-ounce) can Chinese water chestnuts, drained

1 head Chinese cabbage, washed and chopped

4 garlic cloves, minced

1 tablespoon minced fresh ginger

1 teaspoon salt

1 teaspoon cornstarch

1 cup water, divided

Per serving: Calories 118; Fat 1g; Protein 6g; Carbohydrates 25g; Fiber 4g; Sodium 523mg

1. In the slow cooker, combine the broccoli, carrots, water chestnuts, cabbage, garlic, ginger, and salt.

2. In a small bowl, whisk together the cornstarch and ¼ cup of water until well combined.

3. Add the cornstarch mixture and the remaining ¾ cup of water to the slow cooker.

4. Cook on low for 8 hours.

Tip: *Feel free to add in or swap out the vegetables. Other choices might be baby corn, bok choy, or mushrooms.*

Ruby Red Roasted Beets

SERVES 6 | **COOK TIME** 8 HOURS | **LOW**

Beets take forever to roast in a hot oven. Using the slow cooker means you can just set them and forget them. Serve these beets warm with a bit of butter or a drizzle of olive oil, or chill them and cut them into wedges or cubes and add them to salads. Paired with mixed greens, a salty cheese like Gorgonzola, a sprinkling of toasted nuts, and a tangy-sweet balsamic vinaigrette, they make a side salad that's special enough for company.

Cooking spray

6 beets, scrubbed well

6 tablespoons olive oil

Aluminum foil

Salt

_____

Per serving: Calories 164; Fat 14g; Protein 2g; Carbohydrates 10g; Fiber 2g; Sodium 77mg

1. Coat the slow cooker with cooking spray.

2. Rub each beet with 1 tablespoon of oil.

3. Wrap each beet in aluminum foil.

4. Place the wrapped beets in the slow cooker.

5. Cook on low for 8 hours, and season with salt before serving.

Tip: Once roasted, the beet skins should slip off easily. Remove the beets from the slow cooker when tender and let sit until cool enough to handle before trying to peel them.

Savory Baked Apples

SERVES 6 | **COOK TIME** 6 HOURS | **LOW**

Unlike the sweet baked apples often served as dessert, these savory apples make a great side dish. While you can use any kind of apple, Granny Smiths hold up best in the slow cooker. We recommend leaving the skins on to help them hold their shape, but feel free to peel the apples first if you prefer.

Cooking spray

6 Granny Smith apples, washed, cored, and sliced

2 tablespoons olive oil

1 teaspoon chopped fresh sage

½ teaspoon dried oregano

½ teaspoon salt

Dash freshly ground black pepper

Per serving: Calories 135; Fat 5g; Protein 1g; Carbohydrates 25g; Fiber 5g; Sodium 195mg

1. Coat the slow cooker with cooking spray.

2. In the slow cooker, combine all the ingredients.

3. Cook on low for 6 hours.

Tip: Depending on your slow cooker, you might be able to cook the apples for longer than 6 hours. However, you don't want them to turn into applesauce (although that might be delicious!), so start checking it at 6 hours.

Stuffed Acorn Squash

SERVES 4 | **COOK TIME** 8 HOURS | **LOW**

Winter squash can take a long time to cook in the oven. Using the slow cooker frees you from having to stick around to monitor it. You can substitute any kind of winter squash you like for the acorn, such as butternut or even pumpkin! Also, while we've filled the acorn squash with a rice mixture in this recipe, it would also be great stuffed with the *Savory Baked Apples* (page 129). Just assemble the baked apple ingredients and cook them directly in the squash halves.

Cooking spray

1 acorn squash, cut in half lengthwise, seeds scooped out and discarded

1 cup cooked brown rice

1 tablespoon chopped dried cranberries

1 tablespoon chopped pecans

1 garlic clove, minced

Leaves from 2 sprigs fresh thyme, finely chopped

1 tablespoon chopped fresh rosemary

½ teaspoon salt

Dash freshly ground black pepper

Per serving: Calories 244; Fat 4g; Protein 5g; Carbohydrates 49g; Fiber 4g; Sodium 296mg

1. Coat the slow cooker with cooking spray.

2. In the slow cooker, place the squash halves cut-side up.

3. In a medium bowl, combine the rice, dried cranberries, pecans, garlic, thyme, rosemary, salt, and pepper.

4. Divide the stuffing mixture between the two squash halves.

5. Cook on low for 8 hours.

Tip: To stabilize the squash halves in the slow cooker, cut a thin slice off the bottom side.

Eggplant in Hoisin Garlic Sauce

SERVES 6 | **COOK TIME** 6 HOURS | **LOW**

When eggplant is slow cooked, it takes on an appealing velvety texture and soaks up the flavors of everything it's cooked with. Here it's tossed with soy sauce, hoisin sauce, ginger, and lots of garlic for a dish that's as good or even better than your favorite Chinese restaurant's version.

Cooking spray

1½ pounds eggplant

4 cloves garlic, minced

2 tablespoons grated fresh ginger

¾ cup water

1½ tablespoons vegan chicken-flavored bouillon

2 tablespoons soy sauce

2 tablespoons hoisin sauce

2 tablespoons brown sugar

½ teaspoon chili paste

2 tablespoons sesame oil

3 scallions, thinly sliced

1. Coat the slow cooker with cooking spray.

2. In the slow cooker, combine all the ingredients except the sesame oil and scallions and stir to mix.

3. Cook on low for 6 hours. Serve hot, drizzled with the sesame oil and garnished with the scallions.

Per serving: Calories 110; Fat 5g; Protein 2g; Carbohydrates 16g; Fiber 5g; Sodium 393mg

Russian Red Cabbage with Apples

SERVES 6 | **COOK TIME** 8 HOURS | **LOW**

This is a delicious twist on regular braised cabbage. It combines red cabbage and apples with a tangy vinegar sauce. Apple cider vinegar is the kind to use here, as it adds a specific taste. If you're vegan, you can swap out the butter for olive oil or vegan margarine.

1 large head red cabbage, washed, cored, and coarsely chopped

2 medium yellow onions, coarsely chopped

3 Granny Smith apples, cored and quartered

2 teaspoons salt

2 cups water

3 tablespoons granulated sugar

⅔ cup apple cider vinegar

6 tablespoons unsalted butter

2 dashes liquid smoke

1. In the slow cooker, stir together all the ingredients.

2. Cook on low for 8 hours.

Per serving: Calories 222; Fat 12g; Protein 2g; Carbohydrates 29g; Fiber 6g; Sodium 884mg

Chiles Rellenos Stuffed with Fresh Mozzarella

SERVES 4 | **COOK TIME** 8 HOURS | **LOW**

Chiles Rellenos is a Mexican stuffed-pepper dish in which the peppers are usually battered and deep fried. This slow cooker vegetarian version is both healthier and easier! It sticks to the classic cheese filling and makes a satisfying meal served alongside rice and beans.

Cooking spray

½ **cup grated fresh mozzarella cheese**

½ **cup (4 ounces) cream cheese, at room temperature**

4 **poblano peppers, tops removed, seeds and membranes scooped out**

Per serving: Calories 198; Fat 15g; Protein 11g; Carbohydrates 6g; Fiber 1g; Sodium 259mg

1. Coat the slow cooker with cooking spray.

2. In a small bowl, mix together the mozzarella cheese and cream cheese.

3. Stuff each pepper with ¼ cup of the cheese mixture.

4. In the slow cooker, place the peppers and cook on low for 8 hours.

Tip: Fresh mozzarella cheese comes packed in liquid and is usually found near the fresh pasta in your local market. If you can't find any, you can use part-skim ricotta cheese instead.

8

Pizzas, Pastas, and Other Grains

Pizza Primer

SERVES 6 | **COOK TIME** 2 TO 3 HOURS | **LOW**

It's true—you can make pizza in your slow cooker. The key is to only cook the pizza for 2 to 3 hours, depending on your slow cooker, and to not use too much dough. Otherwise, the crust is too thick and will overwhelm the rest of the ingredients.

Cooking spray

1 (16-ounce) container premade
    refrigerated pizza dough

1 cup Simmered Marinara Sauce
    (page 27), or store-bought

2 cups shredded mozzarella cheese

Per serving: Calories 486; Fat 31g; Protein 16g; Carbohydrates 38g; Fiber 4g; Sodium 747mg

1. Coat the slow cooker with cooking spray.

2. Press the dough into the bottom of the slow cooker until it's just touching the edges. Make sure that it's only about ¼ inch thick. Pinch off any excess dough and save it for another use.

3. Spread the sauce on top of the dough, leaving a ½-inch border of dough all around.

4. Top with the cheese.

continued >

5. Cook on low for 2 hours and check the pizza. If the dough is still uncooked, let the pizza cook for another hour.

6. Use a spatula to remove the pizza from the slow cooker and place it on a cutting board before slicing.

Tip: *Try different types of dough to see which you like best. Some people prefer the kind that comes in a refrigerator can, while others prefer the kind that comes in a bag. Either way, you'll probably have some dough left over.*

Mexican Pizza

SERVES 6 | **COOK TIME** 2 TO 3 HOURS | **LOW**

This pizza is as easy as making nachos. Add additional toppings as you like, such as diced red bell peppers or jalapeños, sliced black olives, tomatoes, or soy chorizo. Top with *Custom-Designed Salsa* (page 189) or *Great Guacamole* (page 190) before serving.

Cooking spray

1 (16-ounce) container premade
   refrigerated pizza dough

1 cup refried beans

½ cup shredded Cheddar cheese

½ cup shredded pepper jack cheese

Per serving: Calories 544; Fat 36g; Protein 16g; Carbohydrates 39g; Fiber 5g; Sodium 722mg

1. Coat the slow cooker with cooking spray.

2. Press the dough into the bottom of the slow cooker until it's just touching the edges. Make sure that it's only about ¼ inch thick. Pinch off any excess dough and save it for another use.

3. Spread the refried beans on top of the dough, leaving a ½-inch border all around.

4. Top with the cheeses.

continued >

5. Cook on low for 2 hours and check the pizza. If the dough is still uncooked, let the pizza cook for another hour.

6. Use a spatula to remove the pizza from the slow cooker, and place it on a cutting board before slicing.

Tip: *If your refried beans are too thick to spread, mix them with a little water (about 2 tablespoons) to thin them out.*

Spinach, Swiss, and Mushroom Pizza

SERVES 6 | **COOK TIME** 2 TO 3 HOURS | **LOW**

Spinach, Swiss cheese, and mushrooms make a classic combination that's even better on a pizza. You can substitute another type of cheese, or other dark, leafy greens such as chard or kale, for the spinach.

Cooking spray

1 (16-ounce) container premade refrigerated pizza dough

2 tablespoons olive oil

1 garlic clove, minced

½ cup sliced mushrooms

1 cup tightly packed fresh spinach

2 cups shredded Swiss cheese

Per serving: Calories 544; Fat 39g; Protein 15g; Carbohydrates 35g; Fiber 3g; Sodium 442mg

1. Coat the slow cooker with cooking spray.

2. Press the dough into the bottom of the slow cooker until it's just touching the edges. Make sure that it's only about ¼ inch thick. Pinch off any excess dough and save it for another use.

3. Brush the olive oil onto the crust, leaving a ½-inch border all around, and sprinkle the garlic over the top.

4. Scatter the mushrooms and spinach over the crust.

5. Top with the cheese.

6. Cook on low for 2 hours and check the pizza. If the dough is still uncooked, let the pizza cook for another hour.

7. Use a spatula to remove the pizza from the slow cooker, and place it on a cutting board before slicing.

Mexican Pasta

SERVES 6 | **COOK TIME** 8 HOURS | **LOW**

This south-of-the-border version of mac and cheese uses cooked macaroni. This way you can leave the sauce cooking all day and just add the pasta in the last hour. Feel free to substitute a different shape of pasta, or add additional vegetables like diced tomatoes, corn, or roasted green chiles if you like.

Cooking spray

3 cups whole milk

1 teaspoon salt

3 tablespoons diced red or green bell pepper

½ teaspoon chili powder

½ cup Custom-Designed Salsa (page 189), or store-bought

1½ cups shredded Mexican cheese blend

3 cups cooked elbow macaroni

Per serving: Calories 351; Fat 14g; Protein 17g; Carbohydrates 39g; Fiber 2g; Sodium 747mg

1. Coat the slow cooker with cooking spray.

2. In the slow cooker, stir together the milk, salt, bell pepper, chili powder, salsa, and cheese.

3. Cook on low for 7 hours.

4. Stir in the macaroni and cook on low for 1 more hour.

Tip: If the sauce is too thin, add in ¼ cup mashed potato flakes to thicken it up. If it's too thick, thin it out with ¼ cup of milk.

Long Cooking Lasagna

SERVES 6 | **COOK TIME** 6 HOURS | **LOW**

Between precooking noodles, assembling the lasagna, and cooking it for an hour or more in the oven, lasagna seems like a dish that's only doable on a lazy Sunday afternoon. Here we layer uncooked lasagna noodles with marinara sauce, cheese, and veggies and let it cook unattended all day. You can leave out the spinach and the mushrooms, if you like, or swap them for other vegetables like kale or zucchini. Be sure and set the actual cooking time for 6 hours and then let your slow cooker keep it warm for you if you get home later than that.

Cooking spray

24 ounces Simmered Marinara Sauce (page 27), or store-bought, divided

18 lasagna noodles (not the no-boil kind)

2 cups water

1 (16-ounce) container whole-milk ricotta cheese

1 cup firmly packed fresh spinach

1 cup sliced mushrooms

1 cup diced tomatoes

1 (8-ounce) ball fresh mozzarella cheese, grated

2 ounces Parmesan cheese, finely grated

1. Coat the slow cooker with cooking spray.

2. On the bottom of the crock, spread about ¼ cup of marinara sauce.

3. Place one layer of lasagna noodles on top of the sauce. You may need to break them in order to get them to fit in the crock.

4. In a large bowl, stir together the remaining marinara sauce and the water.

continued >

Per serving: Calories 392; Fat 22g; Protein 26g; Carbohydrates 24g; Fiber 4g; Sodium 934mg

Long Cooking Lasagna, continued

5. Alternate layers of marinara sauce mixture, ricotta cheese, spinach, mushrooms, tomatoes, and pasta until all the ingredients are used.

6. Sprinkle the mozzarella and Parmesan cheeses on top.

7. Cook on low for 6 hours or until the noodles are cooked through.

Stroganoff Sans Beef

SERVES 6 | **COOK TIME** 8 HOURS | **LOW**

Lots of mushrooms in a creamy sauce make this vegetarian version of the classic beef stroganoff perfectly satisfying for both vegetarians and meat eaters alike. Serve it over cooked noodles or over cooked brown rice, bulgur, quinoa, or any other starchy side you like.

3 cups sliced mushrooms

3 garlic cloves, minced

1 onion, halved and then thinly sliced

3 cups Vegetable Broth (page 26), or store-bought

2 teaspoons smoked paprika

1 teaspoon salt

¼ cup sour cream

¼ cup fresh or frozen (and thawed) peas

1. In the slow cooker, stir together the mushrooms, garlic, onion, broth, paprika, and salt.

2. Cook on low for 8 hours.

3. Stir in the sour cream and peas and cook on low for 15 more minutes.

Tip: *This dish freezes well, but only if you omit the sour cream. You can stir in the sour cream after defrosting.*

Per serving: Calories 64; Fat 3g; Protein 5g; Carbohydrates 6g; Fiber 1g; Sodium 778mg

Rice with Green Chiles

SERVES 6 | **COOK TIME** 8 HOURS | **LOW**

This recipe makes a great party side dish since it makes enough for a crowd. You can spice it up by adding *Homemade Hot Pepper Sauce* (page 183) or store-bought hot sauce, or make it cheesy by mixing in ¼ cup of Parmesan cheese just before serving.

Cooking spray

4 cups uncooked long-grain white rice

1 cup sliced scallions (white and green parts)

1 (4-ounce) can diced green chiles

8 cups Vegetable Broth (page 26), or store-bought

Salt

1. Coat the slow cooker with cooking spray.

2. In the slow cooker, combine all the ingredients.

3. Cook on low for 8 hours and season with salt before serving.

Per serving: Calories 513; Fat 3g; Protein 16g; Carbohydrates 102g; Fiber 2g; Sodium 1,102mg

Arroz con Frijoles

SOY-FREE

GLUTEN-FREE

NUT-FREE

VEGAN

SERVES 6 | **COOK TIME** 8 HOURS | **LOW**

Rice and beans is a classic Mexican side dish that combines two of that cuisine's most reliable staples. Usually the beans are cooked separately and then added to the rice, but by using the slow cooker, you can consolidate those two steps. To make this a complete meal, add some vegetables like zucchini or other squash in the last hour of cooking.

2 cups dried pinto beans, soaked overnight

2 cups uncooked long-grain white rice

7 cups Vegetable Broth (page 26), or store-bought

1 cup tomato juice

1 (6-ounce) can tomato paste

1 tablespoon garlic powder

1 tablespoon onion powder

1 teaspoon chili powder

1 teaspoon salt

1. In the slow cooker, stir together all the ingredients except the salt.

2. Cook on low for 8 hours.

3. Stir in the salt just before serving.

Tip: *You can use black beans in this recipe. They will taste just as good, but they might discolor the rice.*

Per serving: Calories 533; Fat 3g; Protein 26g; Carbohydrates 100g; Fiber 13g; Sodium 1,431mg

Perfect Paella

SERVES 6 | **COOK TIME** 8 HOURS | **LOW**

Paella, usually made with seafood and sausage, is a hallmark of Spanish cuisine. A layer of rice topped with an assortment of savory items, it manages to be both impressive and practical at the same time. Highly prized—and expensive—saffron is what gives traditional paella its golden hue, but we've substituted turmeric because it is more widely available and more likely to be in your pantry. You can simply leave it out if you don't have any on hand.

Cooking spray

2 garlic cloves, minced

1 cup marinated artichoke hearts, quartered

1 cup sliced carrots

1 bunch asparagus, ends trimmed, cut into 2-inch pieces

1 cup sliced mushrooms

1 (14.5-ounce) can diced tomatoes with their juices

1 tablespoon ground turmeric

½ teaspoon paprika

2 bay leaves

2 cups uncooked long-grain rice

4 cups Vegetable Broth (page 26), or store-bought

1 cup frozen (and thawed) peas

Salt

1. Coat the slow cooker with cooking spray.

2. In the slow cooker, combine all the ingredients except the peas.

3. Cook on low for 8 hours.

4. Add the peas on top of the rice and cook on low for 15 more minutes.

Tip: *If you wish, you can slice up some vegetarian sausage and add it to the dish in the last hour.*

Per serving: Calories 407; Fat 10g; Protein 11g; Carbohydrates 64g; Fiber 5g; Sodium 715mg

Millet and Mushroom Stew

SERVES 6 | **COOK TIME** 8 HOURS | **LOW**

Millet is an underrated grain. It's rich in iron, B vitamins, and calcium, and has a pleasing, mild corn flavor. It's also naturally gluten-free. This recipe combines millet with savory vegetables to make a hearty stew.

1 cup uncooked millet

4 cups water

2 yellow onions, cut into wedges or large chunks

4 new red potatoes, quartered

2 carrots, peeled and sliced

1 cup sliced celery

8 ounces sliced mushrooms

2 bay leaves

½ teaspoon dried basil

½ teaspoon dried thyme

Salt

1. In the slow cooker, stir together all the ingredients.

2. Cook on low for 8 hours, and season with salt before serving.

Tip: *To enhance the flavor of the millet, toast it in a dry skillet for about 5 minutes before adding it to the slow cooker. Be careful not to burn it, though!*

Per serving: Calories 259; Fat 2g; Protein 8g; Carbohydrates 54g; Fiber 7g; Sodium 46mg

Black Bean Burritos

SERVES 6 | **COOK TIME** 8 HOURS | **LOW**

Black beans simmered all day with veggie broth, tomatoes, and spices make a great filling for tortillas, and it's a welcome, quick, and healthy meal at the end of a long workday. If you're not vegan, you can add shredded cheese to the burritos before rolling them.

Cooking spray

2 cups dried black beans, soaked overnight

4 cups Vegetable Broth (page 26), or store-bought

1 (14.5-ounce) can diced tomatoes, drained

2 garlic cloves, chopped

1 red bell pepper, diced

1 tablespoon ground cumin

1 teaspoon chipotle chili powder

6 burrito-size flour tortillas

Salt

Per serving: Calories 322; Fat 3g; Protein 20g; Carbohydrates 56g; Fiber 13g; Sodium 529mg

1. Coat the slow cooker with cooking spray.

2. In the slow cooker, stir together all the ingredients except the tortillas.

3. Cook on low for 8 hours.

4. To serve, place a tortilla on each of 6 plates. Spoon ½ cup of the bean mixture in the middle of each tortilla and spread it down through the center. Lightly season each mixture with salt. Fold each end over to cover the edges of the beans by about 1½ inches. Roll up the tortilla along the long edge.

Tip: *You can add some hot cooked rice to the burritos along with the bean mixture, if you wish. Just adjust the mixture so that it totals ½ cup, or the burrito will be too full.*

Greek Bulgur and Lentils

SERVES 6 | **COOK TIME** 8 HOURS | **LOW**

Bulgur is the cracked and partially cooked whole-wheat grain. As a whole grain, it's a nutritional powerhouse. A one-cup serving has a full third of a day's fiber requirement, and it is also high in vitamin B_6, magnesium, and potassium. We pair it here with lentils and a handful of flavorful Greek ingredients, to make this dish worthy of a Greek god.

Cooking spray

2 large onions, thinly sliced

1 cup dried lentils, rinsed and sorted

4 cups water

1 cup uncooked bulgur wheat

1½ teaspoons salt

½ teaspoon freshly ground black pepper

¼ cup pitted Kalamata olives, chopped

¼ cup chopped fresh parsley

½ cup crumbled feta cheese

Per serving: Calories 248; Fat 4g; Protein 14g; Carbohydrates 42g; Fiber 15g; Sodium 783mg

1. Coat the slow cooker with cooking spray.

2. In the slow cooker, stir together the onions, lentils, water, bulgur, salt, and pepper.

3. Cook on low for 8 hours.

4. Just before serving, stir in the olives, parsley, and feta cheese.

Tip: Serve this warm, on its own, or wrapped in a tortilla. It's also great cold as a salad.

New Year's Day Black-Eyed Peas

SERVES 6 | **COOK TIME** 8 HOURS | **LOW**

Southern tradition calls for a person to eat at least 365 black-eyed peas on New Year's Day to ensure a lucky year. You can eat this healthy and delicious dish every day and feel lucky all year long. Serve it with rice and greens for a traditional Southern meal.

1 pound dried black-eyed peas, soaked overnight

1 small onion, diced

1 red bell pepper, diced

2 garlic cloves

6 cups water

1 vegetarian bouillon cube

Dash liquid smoke

1 bay leaf

1. In the slow cooker, stir together all the ingredients.

2. Cook on low for 8 hours.

Tip: To make this into "Texas Caviar," add Mexican inspiration, such as corn and diced avocado, right before serving, and serve it with tortilla chips.

Per serving: Calories 71; Fat 1g; Protein 4g; Carbohydrates 13g; Fiber 3g; Sodium 25mg

Smoky Farro with Peas

SERVES 6 | **COOK TIME** 8 HOURS | **LOW**

Farro is a delicious, yet often overlooked, healthy grain that has roots in the ancient cuisines of both Egypt and Rome and has been a part of Italian cuisine for centuries. With the surging interest in whole grains, Americans have recently "discovered" farro, and you'll find it on trendy restaurant menus everywhere. This version is characterized by a smoky flavor thanks to a dash of liquid smoke. If you're not a vegan, you can serve this topped with a fried egg.

Cooking spray

1 cup uncooked farro

2 ½ cups Vegetable Broth (page 26), or store-bought

2 dashes liquid smoke

1 bay leaf

2 tablespoons chopped fresh parsley

½ cup chopped yellow onion

¼ teaspoon freshly ground black pepper

½ teaspoon dried thyme

1 cup thawed frozen peas

Salt

Per serving: Calories 154; Fat 1g; Protein 8g; Carbohydrates 28g; Fiber 5g; Sodium 320mg

1. Coat the slow cooker with cooking spray.

2. In the slow cooker, stir together the farro, broth, liquid smoke, bay leaf, parsley, onion, black pepper, and thyme.

3. Cook on low for 8 hours.

4. Add the peas and cook on low for 15 more minutes.

5. Before serving, add salt to taste.

Tip: *There are several different types of farro—einkorn, emmer, and spelt— but any of them will work in this recipe.*

Barley Chickpea Risotto

SERVES 6 | **COOK TIME** 8 HOURS | **LOW**

Typically, risotto is made by standing over a pan and adding broth a little bit at a time, stirring continuously, as the rice absorbs the broth. In this recipe, the slow cooker does all the work for you! The result is the classic creamy taste you expect from risotto with the hands-off convenience of a slow cooker. The addition of barley gives this risotto an extra boost of nutrition.

Cooking spray

3 carrots, peeled and chopped

3 garlic cloves, minced

½ head cauliflower, cut into small florets

½ small yellow onion, finely chopped

Leaves from 4 sprigs fresh thyme, chopped

1¼ cups uncooked pearl barley, rinsed

1 cup dried chickpeas, soaked overnight

1 cup uncooked long-grain white rice

2½ cups Vegetable Broth (page 26), or store-bought

1¼ cups water

¼ teaspoon freshly ground black pepper

1½ tablespoons freshly squeezed lemon juice

⅓ cup grated Parmesan cheese

3 tablespoons chopped fresh parsley

Per serving: Calories 468; Fat 6g; Protein 20g; Carbohydrates 84g; Fiber 14g; Sodium 494mg

1. Coat the slow cooker with cooking spray.

2. In the slow cooker, stir together the carrots, garlic, cauliflower, onion, thyme, barley, chickpeas, rice, broth, water, and black pepper.

3. Cook on low for 8 hours.

4. Just before serving, stir in the lemon juice, Parmesan, and parsley.

Tip: If you'd like to make this vegan, omit the cheese and substitute ¼ cup nutritional yeast flakes instead.

Tex-Mex Quinoa

SERVES 6 | **COOK TIME** 8 HOURS | **LOW**

This light, flavorful, and nutritious dish is loaded with protein. Take it to a potluck and not only will you be assured of something vegetarian to eat, but you'll get raves from everyone there. Using already cooked black beans prevents them from turning the whole dish black. If you're not vegan, top it with shredded cheese.

Cooking spray

1½ cups uncooked quinoa, well rinsed

1 (14.5-ounce) can diced tomatoes with their juices

2 cups corn kernels

1 cup chopped red bell pepper

1 poblano chile, chopped

1 teaspoon minced garlic

½ cup chopped yellow onion

2 tablespoons chili powder

1½ teaspoons ground cumin

3 cups Vegetable Broth (page 26), or store-bought

2 cups cooked black beans (see page 25)

¼ cup chopped fresh cilantro

1 tablespoon freshly squeezed lime juice

1 teaspoon salt

1. Coat the slow cooker with cooking spray.

2. In the slow cooker, stir together the quinoa, tomatoes, corn, red bell pepper, poblano, garlic, onion, chili powder, cumin, and broth.

3. Cook on low for 8 hours.

4. Stir in the black beans, cilantro, lime juice, and salt and cook on low for 15 more minutes.

Per serving: Calories 462; Fat 5g; Protein 25g; Carbohydrates 83g; Fiber 16g; Sodium 806mg

9

Desserts and Drinks

Pear Applesauce

SERVES 6 | **COOK TIME** 6 HOURS | **LOW**

This applesauce, flavored with ginger, cardamom, and clove, is so much better than anything you'll get from a jar. Eat it plain, warm or chilled, spread on toast, stirred into yogurt or oatmeal, or use it as a topping for ice cream.

Cooking spray

4 medium apples, peeled, cored, and cut into large chunks

4 medium pears, peeled, cored, and cut into large chunks

1 teaspoon freshly squeezed lemon juice

5 teaspoons firmly packed dark brown sugar

1 cinnamon stick

1 teaspoon pure vanilla extract

½ teaspoon ground ginger

½ teaspoon ground cardamom

½ teaspoon ground cloves

Per serving: Calories 143; Fat 0g; Protein 1g; Carbohydrates 37g; Fiber 7g; Sodium 266mg

1. Coat the slow cooker with cooking spray.

2. In the slow cooker, stir together all the ingredients.

3. Cook on low for 6 hours. Remove the cinnamon stick.

4. For a smoother sauce, use an immersion blender or regular blender and process until the sauce reaches your desired texture.

Tip: *If you are using a regular blender, be careful to fill it less than halfway full for each batch since the heat will expand its volume while blending. Also, place a dish towel over the top so that if some does come out, you won't burn yourself.*

Apple Oat Cake

SERVES 6 | **COOK TIME** 6 HOURS | **LOW**

This cake is just the thing to make on a crisp fall day when you've got an abundance of apples. When it's finished cooking, cut it into squares and serve topped with ice cream, caramel sauce, or maple syrup.

Cooking spray

5 apples, peeled and chopped

¼ cup granulated sugar

1 box organic yellow cake mix

¼ cup grapeseed oil (or another neutral-flavored oil, such as safflower or sunflower seed oil)

1 egg (or as directed on cake mix box)

1 cup water

½ cup oats

½ cup (1 stick) unsalted butter, cut into slices

Per serving: Calories 740; Fat 36g; Protein 6g; Carbohydrates 102g; Fiber 5g; Sodium 696mg

1. Coat the slow cooker with cooking spray.

2. In the slow cooker, stir together all the ingredients.

3. Cook on low heat for 6 hours. Let cool a bit before serving.

Tip: Though the recipe does call for a boxed cake mix, make sure you buy a healthy one. Avoid the commercial brands that have partially hydrogenated vegetable oil and other unhealthy, unnatural ingredients. Most major grocery stores carry organic cake mixes near the gluten-free items.

Drunken Apples

SERVES 6 | **COOK TIME** 8 HOURS | **LOW**

This is a delicious, healthy, adults-only dessert that will make a great light finish for just about any meal. Feel free to swap out the orange liqueur for another flavor if you prefer.

Cooking spray

6 apples, cored (peels left on)

½ cup (1 stick) unsalted butter, cut into six pats

¼ cup firmly packed dark brown sugar

1 cup orange flavored liqueur (such as Grand Marnier)

Per serving: Calories 359; Fat 16g; Protein 1g; Carbohydrates 31g; Fiber 4g; Sodium 112mg

1. Coat the slow cooker with cooking spray.

2. In the slow cooker, place each apple stem-side up. Top each apple with one pat of butter and 2 teaspoons of brown sugar.

3. Cook on low for 7 hours.

4. Pour the orange liqueur over the apples and cook on low for 1 more hour.

Tip: *Although Granny Smith apples hold up especially well for cooking, you can use any kind you like in this recipe because the skins are left on.*

Perfect Peach Cobbler

SERVES 6 | **COOK TIME** 6 HOURS | **LOW**

Peach cobbler is an American classic, and the slow cooker is the perfect appliance for cooking it. Use up all those summer peaches with this recipe. If you're not vegan, serve it with a scoop of vanilla ice cream on top.

Cooking spray

6 cups fresh peaches, pitted and sliced (leave the skins on or peel them, depending on your preference)

½ cup firmly packed dark brown sugar

1 tablespoon ground cinnamon

1 (16-ounce) can refrigerator biscuits

½ cup granulated sugar

Per serving: Calories 417; Fat 11g; Protein 7g; Carbohydrates 77g; Fiber 4g; Sodium 785mg

1. Coat the slow cooker with cooking spray.

2. Layer the peaches in the bottom of the slow cooker.

3. Sprinkle the brown sugar and cinnamon over the peaches.

4. Lay the biscuits on top of the peaches.

5. Sprinkle the granulated sugar on top of the biscuits.

6. Cook on low for 6 hours.

Tip: This recipe works well with almost any stone fruit. Try it with cherries, nectarines, or plums.

Date Night Chocolate Pudding Cake

SERVES 6 | **COOK TIME** 4 HOURS | **LOW**

Similar to the molten lava cake that has become ubiquitous on restaurant menus, this rich chocolate dessert simply oozes chocolatey goodness. The key to success for this recipe is to not stir the batter and water together once they are in the slow cooker. Serve with a dollop of whipped cream or, if you're vegan, a dollop of whipped coconut cream.

Cooking spray

Parchment paper

1 cup unbleached all-purpose flour

1 cup granulated sugar, divided

½ cup unsweetened Dutch-processed cocoa powder, divided

2 teaspoons baking powder

¼ teaspoon salt

½ cup whole milk

4 tablespoons unsalted butter, melted

1 large egg yolk

2 teaspoons pure vanilla extract

½ cup semisweet chocolate chips

1 cup boiling water

Per serving: Calories 405; Fat 16g; Protein 5g; Carbohydrates 67g; Fiber 4g; Sodium 165mg

1. Coat the slow cooker with cooking spray.

2. Line the bottom with parchment paper and coat it again with cooking spray.

3. In a medium bowl, combine the flour, ½ cup of sugar, ¼ cup of cocoa powder, baking powder, salt, milk, butter, egg yolk, vanilla, and chocolate chips. Mix well. Scrape the batter into the bottom of the slow cooker and spread it to the edges.

continued ›

Date Night Chocolate Pudding Cake, continued

4. In a small bowl, whisk together the remaining ½ cup of sugar and the remaining ¼ cup of cocoa powder. Sprinkle the mixture on top of the batter.

5. Pour the boiling water over the whole thing in the slow cooker. Do not stir.

6. Cook on low heat for 4 hours.

Tip: *You can customize this cake by adding ¼ cup of fresh dark cherries, chopped walnuts, or any other ingredients you like to the batter.*

Chocolate Bread Pudding with Chocolate Chips

SERVES 6 | **COOK TIME** 4 HOURS | **LOW**

This classic comfort-food dessert is perfect for the slow cooker, and it's a great way to use up slightly stale bread. This version uses challah or egg bread, but you can substitute any kind of soft bread. The bread is soaked in a milk and egg custard that has been sweetened with sugar and flavored with vanilla extract and cocoa powder.

Cooking spray

1 loaf challah or egg bread, cubed

½ cup raisins

½ cup semisweet chocolate chips

2 cups whole milk

3 medium eggs

½ cup granulated sugar

⅓ cup unsweetened Dutch-
processed cocoa powder

1 teaspoon pure vanilla extract

Per serving: Calories 511; Fat 17g; Protein 15g; Carbohydrates 81g; Fiber 4g; Sodium 203mg

1. Coat the slow cooker with cooking spray.

2. Place the bread cubes and raisins in the slow cooker.

3. Sprinkle the chocolate chips over the top.

4. In a medium bowl, whisk together the milk, eggs, sugar, cocoa powder, and vanilla.

5. Pour the egg mixture over the bread. Stir gently.

6. Cook on low for 4 hours.

Tip: When cooking in a slow cooker it is especially important to use pure vanilla extract rather than the cheap imitation stuff, which can develop an off flavor after hours in the slow cooker.

Coconut Milk and Tapioca Pudding

SERVES 4 | **COOK TIME** 4 HOURS | **LOW** | **CHILLING TIME** 2 HOURS

Tapioca pearls are simmered in coconut milk and sweetened with stevia, a natural, sugar-free sweetener, for a vegan version of this comfort food classic. Since this version doesn't contain any eggs, the consistency will be thinner after cooking and it will need a couple of hours of chilling to set.

½ **cup small pearl tapioca**

4 **cups sugar-free vanilla coconut milk**

1 **teaspoon pure vanilla extract**

2 **packets powdered stevia**

Per serving: Calories 623; Fat 57g; Protein 6g; Carbohydrates 30g; Fiber 6g; Sodium 36mg

1. In the slow cooker, stir together all the ingredients.

2. Cook on low for 4 hours.

3. Transfer the pudding to a large bowl, cover with plastic wrap, and let it cool in the refrigerator for 2 hours before serving.

Cheesecake in a Jar

SERVES 5 | **COOK TIME** 4 HOURS | **LOW** | **COOLING TIME** 4 HOURS

You probably never even thought of making cheesecake in the slow cooker, but these individual cakes are a cinch. Delicious, beautiful, and delightfully portable, they make perfect holiday gifts. Just wrap them up with a pretty bow and you'll be the hit of the party.

5 half-pint mason jars

FOR THE CRUST:

8 sheets graham crackers

1 teaspoon ground cinnamon

⅓ cup granulated sugar

**4 tablespoons
unsalted butter, melted**

FOR THE FILLING:

**2 (8-ounce) packages cream
cheese, at room temperature**

**1 (14-ounce can) sweetened
condensed milk**

2 large eggs, at room temperature

2 teaspoons pure vanilla extract

Zest of 1 lemon

Per serving: Calories 832; Fat 52g; Protein 17g; Carbohydrates 77g; Fiber 1g; Sodium 598mg

TO MAKE THE CRUST

In a food processor, combine the graham crackers, cinnamon, sugar, and melted butter, and pulse until the mixture is uniform in color and resembles wet sand. Divide the mixture evenly among the mason jars, pressing it down firmly to form crusts.

TO MAKE THE FILLING

1. Wipe out the food processor bowl to get rid of any stray crumbs. Combine the cream cheese, condensed milk, eggs, vanilla, and lemon zest in the bowl and process until smooth. Divide the mixture evenly among the mason jars. Leave the lids off the jars.

continued >

Cheesecake in a Jar, continued

2. Pour 4 cups of water into the slow cooker. Place the mason jars in the slow cooker, making sure they don't touch each other. The water should come about halfway up the sides of the jars. If it doesn't, add more as needed.

3. Cook on low for 4 hours, or until the cakes are cracked on top.

4. Cover the cheesecakes loosely with plastic wrap and chill them in the refrigerator for 3 to 4 hours before serving.

Caramelized Pineapple Upside-Down Cake

SERVES 6 | **COOK TIME** 4 HOURS | **LOW**

In this classic gooey, sweet treat, the pineapple gets browned and caramelized from being on the bottom of the slow cooker, enhancing its natural sweetness. You can actually cut the sugar in half if you prefer a less sweet cake. Top with ice cream, if desired.

Cooking spray

Aluminum foil

5 tablespoons unsalted butter, chilled

¾ cup firmly packed dark brown sugar

8 pineapple rings (from one 20-ounce can), juices reserved

3 tablespoons dark rum (optional)

¾ cup unbleached all-purpose flour

⅔ cup granulated sugar

¾ teaspoon baking powder

½ teaspoon ground cinnamon

¼ teaspoon salt

4 tablespoons unsalted butter, at room temperature

1 large egg, at room temperature

1 large egg yolk, at room temperature

2 tablespoons whole milk

1. Coat the slow cooker with cooking spray. Line the bottom with aluminum foil (using enough so it reaches about 1 inch up the sides of the slow cooker), and coat it again with cooking spray.

2. Cut the chilled butter into small pieces and scatter them in the slow cooker on top of the foil. Sprinkle the brown sugar over the butter pieces. Layer the pineapple rings on top. Drizzle with the rum (if using).

3. In a medium bowl, whisk together the flour, sugar, baking powder, cinnamon, and salt. Add the room temperature butter, egg, egg yolk, and milk to the bowl, and whisk well until the batter is smooth.

continued ›

Per serving: Calories 471; Fat 19g; Protein 4g; Carbohydrates 72g; Fiber 2g; Sodium 237mg

Caramelized Pineapple Upside-Down Cake, continued

4. Pour the batter over the pineapples in the slow cooker and smooth the top with a spatula.

5. Cook on low for 4 hours. Turn off the slow cooker and let the cake sit for 20 minutes.

6. Using the foil, carefully lift the cake out of the slow cooker and invert it onto a plate. Alternatively, carefully invert the slow cooker insert onto a plate.

Tip: *Canned pineapple works better than fresh here, as fresh pineapple tends to be too dry.*

Vegan Chocolate Peanut Butter Cake

SERVES 6 | **COOK TIME** 4 HOURS | **LOW**

No one will believe that this rich, decadent cake is vegan! It's fudgy and full of creamy peanut butter flavor. You could substitute other dairy-free milks for the coconut milk. Rice milk will add a tad more sweetness, while almond milk will accentuate the nuttiness of the cake.

Cooking spray

Parchment paper

1 cup unbleached all-purpose flour

1¼ cups granulated sugar, divided

3 tablespoons plus ¼ cup unsweetened Dutch-processed cocoa powder

1½ teaspoons baking powder

½ cup coconut milk

2 tablespoons vegan margarine, melted

1 teaspoon pure vanilla extract

½ cup peanut butter (chunky or creamy)

2 cups boiling water

Per serving: Calories 456; Fat 20g; Protein 9g; Carbohydrates 67g; Fiber 4g; Sodium 149mg

1. Coat the slow cooker with cooking spray.

2. Line the bottom with parchment paper and coat it again with cooking spray.

3. In a medium bowl, stir together the flour, ½ cup of sugar, 3 tablespoons of cocoa powder, baking powder, coconut milk, margarine, and vanilla.

4. In a small bowl, beat together the remaining ¾ cup of sugar, the remaining ¼ cup of cocoa powder, and the peanut butter. Spoon the peanut butter mixture over the batter in the slow cooker, and pour the boiling water over the top.

5. Cook on low heat for 4 hours.

Perfect Pound Cake

SERVES 6 | **COOK TIME** 4 HOURS | **LOW**

Because sometimes you want a pound cake, but you don't want to heat up your kitchen by turning on your oven, there is slow cooker pound cake. For added vanilla flavor, split a vanilla bean pod and scrape the seeds into the batter. Serve topped with fresh fruit such as berries, peaches, or apricots and a dollop of whipped cream.

Cooking spray

Parchment paper

2 cups unbleached all-purpose flour

½ teaspoon cream of tartar

¼ teaspoon salt

1 cup (2 sticks) unsalted butter, melted and slightly cooled

1 cup granulated sugar

6 eggs

2 teaspoons pure vanilla extract

Per serving: Calories 616; Fat 36g; Protein 10g; Carbohydrates 66g; Fiber 1g; Sodium 377mg

1. Coat the slow cooker with cooking spray.

2. Line the bottom with parchment paper and coat it again with cooking spray.

3. In a medium bowl, stir together all the ingredients until well combined.

4. Scrape the batter into the slow cooker and smooth the top with a spatula.

5. Cook on low for 4 hours.

Tip: This cake freezes particularly well, because of the high fat content. Wrap it tightly and it will keep for 3 months in the freezer.

Pineapple-Carrot Cake

SERVES 6 | **COOK TIME** 4 HOURS | **LOW**

This rich carrot cake gets its moist sweetness from crushed pineapple. It's also studded with walnuts and spiced with cinnamon and cloves. All that's to say that it's so flavorful, you won't miss the frosting, but you could always add a layer of your favorite cream cheese frosting if you like.

Cooking spray

Parchment paper

2 ½ cups unbleached all-purpose flour

2 teaspoons baking powder

1 teaspoon ground cinnamon

¼ teaspoon ground cloves

¼ cup firmly packed dark brown sugar

1 (8-ounce) can crushed pineapple, half of the juice drained out (and reserved for another use)

1 cup buttermilk

1 teaspoon pure vanilla extract

½ cup raisins

½ cup chopped walnuts

2 cups shredded carrot

1. Coat the slow cooker with cooking spray.

2. Line the bottom with parchment paper and coat it again with cooking spray.

3. In a medium bowl, combine all the ingredients. Scrape the batter into the slow cooker.

4. Cook on low for 4 hours.

Per serving: Calories 368; Fat 7g; Protein 10g; Carbohydrates 68g; Fiber 4g; Sodium 75mg

Stewed Sweet Potatoes and Pineapples

SERVES 6 | **COOK TIME** 8 HOURS | **LOW**

Sweet potatoes are one of those rare vegetables that can bridge the divide between savory side and dessert. Here, they're sweetened with brown sugar and pineapple for a healthy treat. Toasting the pecans before adding them to the slow cooker gives this dish a richer flavor.

Cooking spray

4 sweet potatoes, peeled and chopped

¼ cup firmly packed brown sugar

½ cup pecans, toasted and chopped

1 (8-ounce) can pineapple chunks

Per serving: Calories 544; Fat 34g; Protein 8g; Carbohydrates 68g; Fiber 12g; Sodium 16mg

1. Coat the slow cooker with cooking spray.

2. In the slow cooker, combine all the ingredients.

3. Cook on low for 8 hours.

Tip: *Many sweet potato recipes call for marshmallows, but since most marshmallows are made with gelatin (an animal product), they're not suitable for vegetarians or vegans. Look for vegan marshmallows at health food stores and some supermarkets and, if you like, sprinkle them over the top of the sweet potatoes an hour before the cooking time is up.*

The Best Part of the Apple Pie

SOY-FREE

GLUTEN-FREE

NUT-FREE

VEGAN

SERVES 6 | **COOK TIME** 8 HOURS | **LOW**

If you're one of those people who think the best part of an apple pie is the filling, then you're in luck. This recipe cuts out the middleman and gives you just what you crave—crustless apple pie! If you're not a vegan, serve it with vanilla ice cream.

Cooking spray

1 tablespoon freshly squeezed lemon juice

¼ cup cornstarch

3 cups water

8 cups peeled, thinly sliced apples

2 cups granulated sugar

1 teaspoon ground cinnamon

¼ teaspoon ground nutmeg

½ teaspoon salt

Per serving: Calories 348; Fat 0g; Protein 1g; Carbohydrates 92g; Fiber 4g; Sodium 200mg

1. Coat the slow cooker with cooking spray.

2. In a small bowl, whisk together the lemon juice, cornstarch, and water. Set aside.

3. Place the apples in the slow cooker.

4. Sprinkle the sugar over the apples.

5. Pour the cornstarch mixture over the apples.

6. Add the cinnamon, nutmeg, and salt and stir well.

7. Cook on low for 8 hours.

Leftover Rice Pudding

SERVES 6 | **COOK TIME** 8 HOURS | **LOW**

If you've made too much rice, don't despair. This recipe is a great use for it. Cooked white rice is simmered in milk, sweetened with sugar, studded with raisins, and flavored with vanilla and almond extracts for a warm and comforting sweet treat.

Cooking spray

4 cups whole milk

½ cup granulated sugar

2 cups cooked white rice

1 tablespoon unsalted butter

1 egg

¼ cup raisins

½ teaspoon pure vanilla extract

½ teaspoon almond extract

⅛ teaspoon salt

Per serving: Calories 433; Fat 8g; Protein 11g; Carbohydrates 78g; Fiber 1g; Sodium 151mg

1. Coat the slow cooker with cooking spray.

2. In the slow cooker, combine all the ingredients.

3. Cook on low for 8 hours.

Tip: If there are only adults eating this, consider adding in ¼ cup of rum. Either dark rum or coconut-flavored rum would work.

Vanilla Bean Baked Custard

SERVES 6 | **COOK TIME** 8 HOURS | **LOW**

The smooth, creamy texture and pure and simple vanilla flavor make this baked custard a perfect dessert when you want something satisfying, but unfussy. Serve it on its own or topped with fresh berries or sliced peaches, bananas, or other fruit.

2 cups milk

5 eggs, lightly beaten

⅓ cup superfine sugar

1 teaspoon vanilla extract

Pinch of salt

1 vanilla bean

Per serving: Calories 136; Fat 5g; Protein 7g; Carbohydrates 15g; Fiber 0g; Sodium 117mg

1. In the slow cooker, stir together the milk, eggs, sugar, vanilla extract, and salt.

2. With a sharp knife, split the vanilla bean and scrape the seeds into the milk mixture. Whisk to combine well.

3. Cook on low for 8 hours.

Swedish Glögg

SERVES 12 | **COOK TIME** 8 HOURS | **LOW**

This mulled, spiced wine is a classic Swedish beverage and the perfect cold weather drink. There's no need to use expensive bottles of wine, port, and brandy here, as they will be infused with the fruit and spices.

1 (1.5-liter) bottle dry red wine

1 (1.5-liter) bottle port

1 (750-milliliter) bottle brandy

4 cinnamon sticks

15 cardamom seed pods or
    1 teaspoon whole
    cardamom seeds

24 whole cloves

1 whole orange peel, washed

½ cup dark raisins

1 cup blanched almonds

2 cups granulated sugar

Per serving: Calories 469; Fat 4g; Protein 2g; Carbohydrates 47g; Fiber 0g; Sodium 13mg

1. In the slow cooker, combine all the ingredients.

2. Cook on low for 8 hours.

3. Before serving, strain the glögg and discard the fruit and nuts.

Tip: Because of the long cooking time of this recipe, we've cut back the amount of sugar that is typically used in stovetop glögg. If you prefer a sweeter drink, add more sugar before serving.

Slow Cooked Sangria Coolers

SERVES 12 | **COOK TIME** 8 HOURS | **LOW**

Sangria is a spiced wine typically found in Spain. It's served chilled and is a great drink for warm summer nights. This version cooks all day in the slow cooker and is then served on ice with some sparkling water for a refreshing treat.

1 (750-milliliter) bottle red wine

¼ cup brandy

¼ cup orange-flavored liqueur (such as Grand Marnier)

Juice of 1 small lime

Juice of 1 small lemon

¼ cup granulated sugar

½ orange, washed and thinly sliced

½ lemon, washed and thinly sliced

Ice

1 (330-milliliter) bottle sparkling water (such as Perrier)

Per serving: Calories 114; Fat 0g; Protein 0g; Carbohydrates 8g; Fiber 0g; Sodium 4mg

1. In the slow cooker, combine the red wine, brandy, orange liqueur, lime juice, lemon juice, sugar, orange, and lemon.

2. Simmer on low heat for 8 hours.

3. To serve, fill a large wine glass with ice, and pour in ⅔ to 1 cup of sparkling water. Gently ladle warm sangria into the glass. Wait 2 minutes until chilled, and serve.

Tip: If you prefer a sweeter variation, use lemon-lime soda or ginger ale instead of the sparkling water.

10

Kitchen Staples

Homemade Hot Pepper Sauce

MAKES ABOUT 2½ CUPS | **COOK TIME** 10 MINUTES

A little hot pepper sauce can turn even the blandest dish into a delicious feast. This tomato-based version combines large, flavorful chiles like poblano or New Mexico with the red-hot heat of habaneros, but you can use as many and whatever chiles you like to get the heat level that's just right for your taste.

2 tablespoons grapeseed oil (or another neutral-flavored oil such as safflower or sunflower seed)

1 medium onion, diced

2 large chiles, such as poblano, New Mexico or Anaheim, diced

2 to 4 habanero chiles, or other small hot chile peppers, diced

4 cloves garlic, minced

1 pound tomatoes, diced (about 3 cups)

1 cup distilled white vinegar

2 teaspoons salt

1 to 3 teaspoons sugar

1. In a large saucepan, heat the oil over medium-high heat. Stir in the onion, chiles, and garlic, and cook, stirring frequently, until the onion softens and begins to brown, about 5 minutes.

2. Reduce the heat to medium and stir in the tomatoes, vinegar, salt, and 1 teaspoon sugar. Cook, stirring occasionally, until the tomatoes begin to disintegrate, about 5 minutes.

continued ›

Per cup: Calories 216; Fat 11g; Protein 3g; Carbohydrates 23g; Fiber 3g; Sodium 1,981mg

3. Taste the sauce and stir in more sugar if desired.

4. In a food processor or blender, purée the mixture until smooth. Strain the purée through a fine-meshed sieve set over a bowl, pressing on the solids with the back of a spoon to extract as much of the liquid as possible. Discard the solids and allow the sauce to cool to room temperature before serving. Store in a covered container in the refrigerator for up to 2 weeks.

Tip: The spiciest parts of a chile pepper are the seeds and inner ribs. Remove and discard these before dicing your chiles for a milder version, or leave them in for a spicier version.

Garlic Cashew Cream Sauce

MAKES ½ CUP | **PREPARATION TIME** 3 HOURS (PASSIVE)

Cashews make a great substitute for both cream and cheese as a topping for all sorts of dishes. This simple cashew-based cream sauce can be drizzled over *Black Bean and Spinach Enchiladas* (page 121) or dolloped onto *Smoky Bean Chili* (page 95). Use a little less water to make a spreadable mixture that makes a great substitute for cream cheese on a bagel.

½ cup cashews, soaked for 3 hours and then drained

½ cup water

Juice of ½ lemon

½ teaspoon apple cider vinegar

1 teaspoon salt

1 garlic clove

1 tablespoon grapeseed oil (or another neutral-flavored oil such as safflower or sunflower seed)

1. In a blender set on high speed, combine the cashews, water, lemon juice, vinegar, salt, and garlic and blend until smooth.

2. With the blender running, drizzle in the oil and process until combined.

3. Refrigerate for several hours or until set.

Per serving (2 tablespoons): Calories 121; Fat 11g; Protein 3g; Carbohydrates 6g; Fiber 1g; Sodium 587mg

Triple Sautéed Mushrooms

SERVES 6 | **COOK TIME** 7 MINUTES

These mushrooms are a fantastic topper for just about anything, including baked potatoes, vegetables, pizza, beans, or grains. Use any kind of mushroom you like. Portobellos and creminis add a nice, meaty flavor, while white or button mushrooms are a bit milder.

3 tablespoons olive oil

⅓ pound white mushrooms, sliced

⅓ pound portobello mushrooms, cut into bite-size pieces

⅓ pound cremini mushrooms, sliced

1 garlic clove, minced

1 tablespoon dry red wine

1 tablespoon teriyaki sauce, or more to taste

¼ teaspoon salt

Freshly ground black pepper

Per serving: Calories 82; Fat 7g; Protein 3g; Carbohydrates 3g; Fiber 2g; Sodium 216mg

1. In a large skillet over medium-high heat, heat the olive oil for 2 minutes.

2. Add the mushrooms and sauté for 2 to 3 minutes until they begin to soften.

3. Add the garlic, wine, teriyaki sauce, and salt to the skillet and cook, stirring frequently, until the mushrooms are golden brown, about 5 minutes.

4. Season with black pepper.

Super Seasoning

MAKES ABOUT ¼ CUP | **PREPARATION TIME** 5 MINUTES

Having spice mixes on hand makes cooking flavorful meals a snap. Using this recipe as a base, feel free to play with other spices and seasonings.

2 tablespoons salt

2 teaspoons granulated sugar

½ teaspoon paprika

1 teaspoon onion powder

1 teaspoon garlic powder

½ teaspoon cornstarch

1. In a small bowl, whisk together all the ingredients.

2. Transfer the mixture to an airtight container. It will keep in the pantry for about 1 month or in the freezer for up to 4 months.

Per tablespoon: Calories 14; Fat 0g; Protein 0g; Carbohydrates 3g; Fiber 0g; Sodium 3,489mg

SOY-FREE

GLUTEN-FREE

NUT-FREE

VEGAN

Tahini-Lemon Sauce

MAKES ABOUT 1¾ CUPS | **PREPARATION TIME** 5 MINUTES

Tahini is a ground sesame paste popular in Middle Eastern cooking. Here, it's blended with garlic and lemon to make a tangy sauce that is great on everything from steamed veggies to grilled veggie kabobs.

1 garlic clove

¾ cup tahini

5 tablespoons fresh lemon juice

1 cup water

¾ teaspoon salt

2 tablespoons minced fresh parsley

Pinch of cayenne pepper (optional)

Per ¼ cup: Calories 157; Fat 14g; Protein 5g; Carbohydrates 6g; Fiber 3g; Sodium 282mg

1. Chop the garlic in a food processor. Add the tahini and lemon juice and process to combine. With the processor running, drizzle in the water until it is well combined. Add the salt, parsley, and cayenne pepper (if using) and process to combine.

2. Store in a covered container in the refrigerator until ready to use. Bring to room temperature before serving.

Tip: If the sauce is too thick for your liking, simply stir in a bit more water until the mixture is well combined and the consistency you desire.

Custom-Designed Salsa

MAKES ABOUT 3 CUPS | **PREPARATION TIME** 15 MINUTES

If you've ever struggled to find salsa that is just right for your taste—not too spicy or too bland, not too chunky or too watery—then this recipe is for you. You can tailor the ingredients to your liking and add extra ingredients, like red peppers or mango, if you are so inclined. Or you can even leave out ingredients, like the garlic or cilantro, if you like—it's your recipe!

6 Roma tomatoes, chopped

2 garlic cloves, minced

2 jalapeño peppers, seeded and minced

2 jalapeño peppers, roasted, skinned, and finely chopped

½ sweet yellow onion, finely chopped

1 tablespoon cumin seeds

1 tablespoon extra-virgin olive oil

Juice of 1 lime

Dash chili powder

Dash salt

Dash freshly ground black pepper

¼ cup chopped fresh cilantro

1. In a large bowl, combine all the ingredients.

2. Cover the bowl with plastic wrap and refrigerate for 15 minutes to allow the flavors to blend.

3. Serve chilled. Leftovers will keep in an airtight container in the refrigerator for up to 1 week.

Per cup: Calories 105; Fat 6g; Protein 3g; Carbohydrates 13g; Fiber 4g; Sodium 18mg

Great Guacamole

MAKES ABOUT 2 CUPS | **PREPARATION TIME** 5 MINUTES

Guacamole dates back to the time of the Aztecs, who made a sauce from the fat-rich avocado fruit combined with tomatoes, chiles, onion, and cilantro—very much like the guacamole commonly found today. Lime juice is a modern addition, but it prevents premature browning. Use it as a dip for chips or dollop it onto *Black Bean and Spinach Enchiladas* (page 121), *Smoky Bean Chili* (page 95), or *Black Bean Burritos* (page 150).

2 large, ripe Haas avocados, diced

1 medium tomato, diced

1 tablespoon finely chopped yellow onion

¼ cup minced cilantro

1 serrano or jalapeño chile, seeded and finely diced

2 tablespoons lime juice

½ teaspoon salt

In a medium bowl, mash the avocado to a chunky purée. Add the tomato, onion, cilantro, chile, lime juice, and salt, and stir to mix well. Cover with plastic wrap, pressing the plastic directly onto the guacamole, and chill until ready to serve.

Per ½ cup: Calories 216; Fat 20g; Protein 2g; Carbohydrates 12g; Fiber 7g; Sodium 394mg

Perfect Pesto

MAKES ABOUT 1½ CUPS | **PREPARATION TIME** 5 MINUTES

Homemade pesto is a great flavor booster to have on hand. Toss it with pasta or other cooked grains, swirl it into soups and stews, or mix it into sauces and salad dressings any time you want to add a punch of fresh herb and garlic flavor.

3 cups packed fresh basil leaves

4 garlic cloves

¾ cup grated Parmesan cheese

½ cup extra-virgin olive oil

¼ cup pine nuts

Per ¼ cup: Calories 117; Fat 16g; Protein 6g; Carbohydrates 2g; Fiber 0g; Sodium 168mg

1. In a food processor, blend all the ingredients until smooth.

2. To store the pesto, transfer it to an airtight container. Pour a thin layer of olive oil on top of the pesto, and then seal the container. Refrigerate for up to 10 days or freeze for up to 3 months.

Hummus for Us

MAKES ABOUT 3 CUPS | **PREPARATION TIME** 5 MINUTES

Hummus is a Middle Eastern staple that is the cornerstone of many vegetarian meals. It works great as a dip or stirred into a bowl of lentils. Tahini is a sesame paste that you can find in the international ethnic section of most grocery stores.

2 cups cooked chickpeas
(see page 25)

2 garlic cloves, minced

1½ teaspoons kosher salt

5 tablespoons freshly squeezed
lemon juice

¼ cup water

⅓ cup tahini, stirred

¼ cup extra-virgin olive oil

1. In a food processor, combine all the ingredients.

2. Blend until smooth. The hummus will keep in an airtight container in the refrigerator for up to 1 week.

Per ¼ cup: Calories 199; Fat 10g; Protein 8g; Carbohydrates 22g; Fiber 7g; Sodium 308mg

Best Barbecue Sauce

MAKES ABOUT 2 CUPS | **PREPARATION TIME** 10 MINUTES | **COOK TIME** 30 MINUTES

While it's easy enough to buy a jar of barbecue sauce, it's much more fun (and healthy) to whip up a batch at home.

1 cup prepared yellow mustard

½ cup granulated sugar

¼ cup firmly packed light brown sugar

¾ cup apple cider vinegar

¼ cup water

2 tablespoons chili powder

1 teaspoon freshly ground black pepper

½ teaspoon cayenne pepper

½ teaspoon soy sauce

2 tablespoons unsalted butter

1 tablespoon liquid smoke

1. In a medium saucepan over medium heat, combine all the ingredients.

2. Bring the mixture to a bubble, reduce the heat to low, and let it simmer for 30 minutes.

3. Remove the pan from the heat, stir well, and let the sauce cool to room temperature before serving or storing. It will keep in an airtight container in the refrigerator for up to 1 month.

Per 2 tablespoons: Calories 97; Fat 5g; Protein 3g; Carbohydrates 13g; Fiber 2g; Sodium 31mg

Cleaning and Caring for Your Slow Cooker

Now that you are well acquainted with your slow cooker, here are a few tips and tricks for keeping it at its best.

» Before cleaning, always turn your slow cooker off, unplug it from the electrical outlet, and allow it to cool.

» The lid can be washed in the dishwasher or with hot, soapy water.

» You can remove the stoneware crock and wash it in the dishwasher or with hot, soapy water. Do not use abrasive cleaning compounds or scouring pads. A cloth, sponge, or rubber spatula will usually remove any residue. To remove water spots and other stains, use a nonabrasive cleaner or vinegar.

» As with any fine ceramic, the stoneware and lid will not withstand sudden temperature changes. Do not wash the stoneware with cold water when it is hot.

» The outside of the heating base may be cleaned with a soft cloth and warm, soapy water. Wipe dry. Do not use abrasive cleaners.

» Never immerse the heating base in water or other liquid.

The Dirty Dozen & Clean Fifteen

A nonprofit and environmental watchdog organization called Environmental Working Group (EWG) looks at data supplied by the US Department of Agriculture (USDA) and the Food and Drug Administration (FDA) each year of the best and worst pesticide loads found in commercial crops. You can use these lists to decide which fruits and vegetables to buy organic to minimize your exposure to pesticides and which produce is considered safe enough to skip the organics. This does not mean they are pesticide-free, though, so wash these fruits and vegetables thoroughly.

These lists change every year, so make sure you look up the most recent before you fill your shopping cart. You'll find the most recent lists as well as a guide to pesticides in produce at EWG.org/FoodNews.

2015 DIRTY DOZEN

Apples	Cucumbers	Peaches	Spinach
Celery	Grapes	Potatoes	Strawberries
Cherry tomatoes	Nectarines	Snap peas (imported)	Sweet bell peppers

In addition to the dirty dozen, the EWG added two American food crops laced with particularly toxic pesticides:

Kale/collard greens	Hot peppers

2015 CLEAN FIFTEEN

Asparagus	Cauliflower	Mangoes	Sweet corn
Avocados	Eggplant	Onions	Sweet peas (frozen)
Cabbage	Grapefruit	Papayas	Sweet potatoes
Cantaloupe	Kiwis	Pineapples	

Measurement Conversions

VOLUME EQUIVALENTS (LIQUID)

US STANDARD	US STANDARD (OUNCES)	METRIC (APPROXIMATE)
2 tablespoons	1 fl. oz.	30 mL
¼ cup	2 fl. oz.	60 mL
½ cup	4 fl. oz.	120 mL
1 cup	8 fl. oz.	240 mL
1½ cups	12 fl. oz.	355 mL
2 cups or 1 pint	16 fl. oz.	475 mL
4 cups or 1 quart	32 fl. oz.	1 L
1 gallon	128 fl. oz.	4 L

VOLUME EQUIVALENTS (DRY)

US STANDARD	METRIC (APPROXIMATE)
⅛ teaspoon	0.5 mL
¼ teaspoon	1 mL
½ teaspoon	2 mL
¾ teaspoon	4 mL
1 teaspoon	5 mL
1 tablespoon	15 mL
¼ cup	59 mL
⅓ cup	79 mL
½ cup	118 mL
⅔ cup	156 mL
¾ cup	177 mL
1 cup	235 mL
2 cups or 1 pint	475 mL
3 cups	700 mL
4 cups or 1 quart	1 L

OVEN TEMPERATURES

FAHRENHEIT (F)	CELSIUS (C) (APPROXIMATE)
250°	120°
300°	150°
325°	165°
350°	180°
375°	190°
400°	200°
425°	220°
450°	230°

WEIGHT EQUIVALENTS

US STANDARD	METRIC (APPROXIMATE)
½ ounce	15 g
1 ounce	30 g
2 ounces	60 g
4 ounces	115 g
8 ounces	225 g
12 ounces	340 g
16 ounces or 1 pound	455 g

Index of Recipes by Dietary Label

Index